Haunted
South Carolina

Haunted South Carolina

Ghosts and Strange Phenomena of the Palmetto State

Alan Brown

Illustrations by Marc Radle

STACKPOLE
BOOKS

Published by
STACKPOLE BOOKS
5067 Ritter Road
Mechanicsburg, PA 17055
www.stackpolebooks.com

Printed the United States of America

10 9 8 7 6 5 4 3 2 1

FIRST EDITION

Cover design by Tessa J. Sweigert

Library of Congress Cataloging-in-Publication Data

Brown, Alan, 1950 Jan. 12,–
    Haunted South Carolina : ghosts and strange phenomena of the Palmetto State / Alan Brown ; illustrations by Marc Radle. — 1st ed.
        p.   cm.
    Includes bibliographical references.
    ISBN-13: 978-0-8117-3635-0 (pbk.)
    ISBN-10: 0-8117-3635-0 (pbk.)
    1. Ghosts—South Carolina. 2. Haunted places—South Carolina. I. Title.
BF1472.U6B7433 2010
133.109757—dc22

                                                                        2009032601

To the two veterans in my family—
Paul Quick and Cole Walker.

Contents

Introduction

SOUTH CAROLINA IS KNOWN AS THE PALMETTO STATE. ITS NICKNAME IS
taken from the Sabal palmetto tree, which was added to the state
flag to commemorate Col. William Moultrie's heroic defense of a
palmetto-log fort on Sullivan's Island in Charleston harbor against
the British fleet in 1776. To people interested in the paranormal,
however, South Carolina is noteworthy for another reason—it is
reputed to be one of the most haunted states in the entire South.

Many residents of South Carolina believe that the ghosts said to
walk among the living represent the spiritual residue that has
imprinted itself upon the landscape during the state's violent history. A number of wars have been waged in South Carolina through
the years. Between 1715 and 1717, British colonists defended themselves against several Indian tribes in what is known today as the
Yamasee War, one of the bloodiest Indian campaigns in American
history. Pirates such as Blackbeard and Stede Bonnet terrorized
people living along the coastal areas of South Carolina between
1717 and 1718. Although Charleston was a focal point in the American Revolution, the war extended to other parts of the state as well.
Charleston was captured by British forces in 1781, but colonial
troops under General Nathanael Greene drove the main British
army from South Carolina to Virginia a year later. Leaders of the
South Carolina militia, such as Francis Marion, eventually forced
smaller British units to leave the state as well.

The record of human misery in South Carolina must also take
into account the plight of the state's slaves. Slave markets were a
common sight in the major cities up until the Civil War. By 1860,

approximately 402,000 African Americans were enslaved in South Carolina.

The people of the Palmetto State suffered mightily during the Civil War. Many believe that the Yankee invaders were especially ruthless in South Carolina because the Civil War began there on April 12, 1861, when shore batteries manned by Citadel cadets and Confederate volunteers began shelling Fort Sumter in Charleston harbor. In 1865, Federal troops under the command of William Tecumseh Sherman set fire to many plantations in South Carolina. They also put the capital, Columbia, to the torch. Approximately 25 percent of the Confederate troops from South Carolina were dead by the end of the Civil War.

Nature has also claimed thousands of victims among the people of South Carolina. In the eighteenth and nineteenth centuries, outbreaks of fever took the lives of hundreds of planters and their families living in the Low Country. In 1886, an earthquake measuring 7.5 on the Richter scale caused $6 million worth of damage. In 1989, Hurricane Hugo caused more than $2.8 billion in damage in Charleston and the surrounding area.

Like the typically resilient people of the Southern states, the people of South Carolina have transformed the tragic episodes of their past into a body of folklore that has no rival. The fates of hundreds of slaves, Tories, Southern belles, and Confederate soldiers have been recounted over and over again in the ghost legends of South Carolina. Historic figures such as Confederate general Wade Hampton III and actor Junius Brutus Booth have also been memorialized in South Carolina's ghostlore. After you have read the stories in this volume, I think you will agree that South Carolina's ghost tales are just as integral to the Palmetto State's past as the historical accounts of its battlefields and antebellum homes.

Central South Carolina

THE ATLANTIC COASTAL PLAIN, ALSO KNOWN IN SOUTH CAROLINA AS
the Low Country, is part of the plain that stretches from New York
to Florida. The central portion of the Atlantic Coastal Plain is blanketed by the Pine Barrens. The cities of Columbia, Cheraw, Camden, and Aiken are founded on the sand hills, which form part of
an ancient beach dating back to a time when the land was covered
by oceans. Swamps cover much of the land in the eastern portion
of this region.

The Lake Murray Monster

Lake Murray, which is fed by the Saluda River, covers more than
fifty thousand acres and has roughly five hundred miles of shoreline. The lake is named after William Spencer Murray, an engineer
from New York who was authorized by Congress in 1920 to head a
study for the establishment of a large-scale power grid in the industrial Northeast. Murray and his partner, T. C. Williams, developed a
plan to build three dams to generate power and to maintain a constant flow of water into the Santee River. On September 21, 1927,
work began on what was to become the largest earthen dam in the
world at that time. When the dam was completed on June 30, 1930,
it stood two hundred feet high and ran a distance of a mile and a

half across Lake Murray. Approximately five thousand people had to be relocated to make the dam a reality. In exchange, the local populace received cheap electricity, a beautiful recreation area, and, quite possibly, a lake monster.

The first sighting of the Lake Murray monster occurred in 1933. The beast, affectionately dubbed "Messie" by locals, was observed swimming in the newly created lake by several residents of Irmo and Ballantine. Witnesses described it as being a cross between a snake and something prehistoric. Sightings of the lake monster continued throughout the rest of the twentieth century. Many of the eyewitnesses were professional people, such as doctors, lawyers, and military personnel. The monster has consistently been described as being between forty and sixty feet long, with the head and body of a snake and the tail of an eel.

Lake Murray biologist Lance Harper, who has kept a file of recorded sightings of Messie, admits that a lake that is forty-one miles long and fourteen miles wide is certainly large enough to accommodate a creature of this size. Harper puts a great deal of credence in the testimonies of witnesses because, to his knowledge, none of them were under the influence of drugs or alcohol when they encountered the monster. Although Harper himself has never seen the Lake Murray monster, the large holes he has found in nets placed around the lake have convinced him that some sort of enormous creature—either a large fish such as a sturgeon or a super-sized reptile of some sort—has taken up residence in Lake Murray. Retired U.S. Army general Marvin Corder, who actually saw the monster, is convinced that it is more than just a big fish.

Most of the witnesses have described a big, aquatic beast simply swimming or diving in Lake Murray. A few, however, depict the creature as being highly aggressive. For example, Buddy Browning was fishing from a boat in a small cove with his wife, Shirley, and their friend Kord Brazell when a large, scaly head surfaced from the water and began swimming in their direction whenever their boat approached the spot where the creature was resting. Several times, the beast came so close to the boat that Buddy could discern that it was not a large fish, an eel, or an alligator. "It was unlike anything I ever saw before, and I have been fishing Lake Murray for over twenty years," Buddy said. Shirley said that when the creature tried to climb into the boat, Buddy had to hit it with a paddle to drive it off. Buddy dismissed the possibility that the animal could have been an alligator because alligators are not native to the lake.

Messie launched another attack against fishermen on the lake in October 1996. A caller to radio station WNOK-FM 104.7 told the disc jockey that he was fishing off Shell Island when he saw a fin two feet long rise out of the water. He flipped a lure right in front of the creature, and it bit his fishing rod in half. "All I had left was just the handle grip!" the caller said.

The last reported sighting of the Lake Murray Monster occurred in 2002. A woman was driving across the dam with a friend when they noticed long, flowing ripples radiating out from what they described as a "wavy, curvy, long thing" in the calm water. Later, the driver said that there was nothing else on the lake that could have disturbed the water in that manner.

Not surprisingly, the people of Irmo have benefited financially from the notoriety of their lake monster. T-shirts and hats displaying images of Messie are available at gift shops, gas stations, and restaurants all over town. Visitors can also purchase a fifty-page booklet about the "Loch Murray Monster." Like the Scottish monster from which Lake Murray's creature derived its name, Messie's true identity may never be determined.

Bigfoot Mania in Neeses

Bigfoot sightings in South Carolina are not as common as they are in the Pacific Northwest and western Canada, but they do occur with some regularity. In fact, the Bigfoot Field Researchers Organization included forty-two reported sightings on its Web site in 2007. Probably the most dramatic South Carolina Bigfoot sighting in the twentieth century took place on July 15, 1997, in the small town of Neeses.

A fourteen-year-old boy named Jackie Hutto was inside his house around noon when heard the family dogs barking and howling inside their pen. Thinking that some sort of varmint was skulking around the property, Jackie went outside. He had only walked a few feet before he saw something that caused him to stop "dead in his tracks." A large, man-like creature approximately eight feet tall was attempting to pull down one side of the dog pen. In an interview given later, Jackie described the beast as being covered with black hair everywhere but his face, chest, and knees. He also said that the creature had a large stomach and discolored teeth that looked like "baby blocks."

Jackie stood rooted to the spot, staring in amazement at the bizarre animal, until it stopped trying to tear down the pen and turned its head in his direction. When it dawned on the boy that he was standing face-to-face with a genuine monster, he spun on his heels and ran back towards the house. Apparently, the creature was just as frightened by Jackie, because it dropped the section of wire fence it was holding and lumbered into the woods. Just before Jackie reached the house, his brother, David, was walking out the front door to see what all the commotion was about. He saw the monster for a few brief moments just as it entered the forest.

Fully aware that they had just witnessed something extraordinary, the two young men decided to notify the local newspaper. Their credibility came into question after their story was published in the *Orangeburg Times and Democrat* because David identified his brother Jackie as a twenty-three-year-old woman. When Jackie Hutto's true identity came to light, the boys explained that they were just trying to protect their anonymity.

Bigfoot mania spread like wildfire through South Carolina following the publication of the story of the Hutto brothers' weird encounter on July 15. Art Dent, the owner of Dog City Paint and Body Shop, displayed an airbrushed "Big Foot Welcome Center" sign outside his establishment. After the excitement over the Hutto brothers' sighting died down, Neeses became just another small town in South Carolina. However, from the point of view of cryptozoologists, the Neeses encounter has provided proof that the Northwest is not the only part of the United States that Bigfoot calls home.

Civil War Ghosts at the Longstreet Theater

Many theaters have at least one resident ghost, but the Longstreet Theater on the campus of the University of South Carolina in Columbia has a better reason than most for being haunted. The theater was originally designed as a chapel and auditorium. Before construction was finally completed in 1855, the roof was blown off twice; in addition, the acoustics had to be completely overhauled several times. The theater, which bears a close resemblance to a Roman temple, was used as a hospital during the Civil War. Following the war, the building became a temporary home to the state legislature. Between 1870 and 1887, the building housed the arsenal and armory for the inspector general of South Carolina. In 1888, it became the university's science building. Five years later, it was converted into a gymnasium. The building was transformed one last time in 1976, when its acoustics problems were finally solved and it became the Longstreet Theater. Named after a controversial jurist, writer, and educator named Augustus B. Longstreet, the four-story building has 312 seats and a circular stage. If the legends can be believed, the Longstreet Theater not only supports the university's theater and dance program—it also provides a home for a host of ghosts.

Ghostly activity in the form of strange noises and disembodied footsteps in deserted hallways has been reported for years in the Longstreet Theater. Theater professor Ann Dreher said that "you can just feel the vibrations." However, the most seemingly haunted place in the theater is undoubtedly the three-chamber Green Room, which served as a hospital morgue during the Civil War. Dr. Thorne Compton, former chair of the Department of Theater and Dance, said that "it gets cold and creepy down there at night." People who have been in the Green Room by themselves have experienced cool breezes and an overwhelming sense of fear. Others have felt unseen eyes staring at them from the shadowy recesses of the room. On several occasions, a person has been seen sitting in the hall close to the theater. Within a few seconds, the strange figure disappears.

Stories of the Longstreet Theater's ghosts have been told for so long at USC that many students refuse to be in the Green Room alone. Anne Dreher has tried to ease her students' fears by assuring them that most people have nothing to be afraid of in the Green Room. "I love to tease students and tell them the ghosts are real friendly unless you're a Yankee," Dreher said.

The Third-Eye Man of USC

The first sighting of the University of South Carolina's "Third-Eye Man" occurred on November 12, 1949, at 10:43 P.M. Two male students were walking down the street in the vicinity of the Longstreet Theater when they saw a man wearing what appeared to be a silver suit pry open a manhole cover at the corner of Sumter and Green streets. As the strange figure climbed into the sewer, he pulled the manhole cover back over the hole. One of the boys, Christopher Nichols, was a reporter for the school newspaper, the *Gamecock*. As soon as he returned to his room, he began working on an article about the creature he dubbed "the Sewer Man."

Interest in the Sewer Man persisted for a few weeks and then died down. The bizarre creature returned with a vengeance six months later. On April 7, 1950, a policeman was patrolling the campus late in the evening when he found the mutilated remains of two chickens on the loading docks of the Longstreet Theater. Shaking his head in disgust, he walked over to his car and phoned in his grisly discovery to the police station. He returned to the scene of the crime and was shocked to see a man dressed in silver bent over one of the chicken carcasses. Startled, the policeman shined his flashlight in the face of the strange man. The policeman was horrified by what he saw. Not only was the figure's face oddly colored and disfigured, but in the middle of his forehead was a third eye! The terrified officer rushed back to his squad car and called for backup. When the policemen arrived at the Longstreet Theater, all they found were a few bones and feathers. After the patrolman who reported the intruder finally calmed down, he repeated his story to his colleagues, but he was unable to convince them that what he saw in the dim light of his flashlight was more than just his imagination.

Although rumors of the Third-Eye Man circulated throughout the 1950s, his existence was relegated to campus lore. Then one October night in the late 1960s, a group of fraternity boys took three pledges to the steam tunnels underneath the university for an initiation ritual. They had just rounded the corner when a silvery figure that appeared to be crippled stepped out of the shadows. In his hand, he held a lead pipe in a very menacing way. Suddenly, the strange man charged the fraternity boys. At that moment, the young

men realized that the Third-Eye Man was more than just a campus myth. Screaming, they spun around and ran back to the opening of the tunnel. The Third-Eye Man managed to tackle one of the pledges, inflicting minor cuts on his face and hands. Two of the older fraternity boys who had escaped unharmed contacted the police department. A thorough search was conducted of all the tunnels, but the Third-Eye Man was gone. To prevent further injuries inside the steam tunnels, the administration had all but the maintenance entrances sealed.

Marc Minsker, a graduate student in English at the University of South Carolina, says that sightings of the Third-Eye Man diminished in the 1980s and 1990s for two reasons. First, the campus police are reluctant to enter the steam tunnels. Second, students who venture into these forbidden regions of the university have been threatened with suspension. As a result, the mystery of the Third-Eye Man continues to deepen with each passing year.

Mystery of the Swamp Girl

One of the world's most popular and prevalent ghost stories is the tale of the phantom hitchhiker. Hundreds of variants of the story can be found throughout the world. As a general rule, the story focuses on a young woman in a white dress who is hitchhiking along a lonely road at night. A driver, usually male, stops his car and asks her where she is bound. She replies that she is going home, and she gives him the street address. He tells the young lady that he is headed in the same direction and offers her a ride. She climbs into the backseat and says nothing the entire way. When the driver arrives at the address the girl gave him, he turns around, and she is gone. He walks up to the house and speaks to an elderly woman, who informs him that her daughter was killed on that very road years before. Every year on the anniversary of her death, someone picks up a girl and brings her to this address. Rosemary Ellen Guiley, author of *The Encyclopedia of Ghosts and Spirits*, says that the story most likely originated in Europe and was brought over to the United States by immigrants. The story of South Carolina's Swamp Girl is one of those variants that retains the basic structure of the original story, but also contains elements reflecting the geographical area in which it is told.

According to most of the versions told in central South Carolina, one rainy, foggy night, a man driving through dense swampland on a dark stretch of highway between Sumter and Columbia spies a young woman standing on the Sumter side of the Wateree River Bridge. She is usually described as wearing a silvery-gray dress and carrying a canvas travel bag. She climbs into the backseat and tells him that she needs to be taken to a specific address on Pickens Street in Columbia to tend to her ailing mother. Just before the car reaches the Columbia side of the bridge, the man turns around to ask her a question, and she is gone. In one version dating back to the 1950s, a man and woman pick up the girl. After she vanishes, the woman becomes so distraught that her husband drives her directly to the hospital in Columbia. While his wife is being treated, the husband drives to the Pickens Street address, where the owner of the house informs him that she was the sister of the girl on the bridge, who was killed in an automobile accident on the swamp road just after the Wateree River Bridge was opened. She returns to the site of the accident every year on the anniversary of her death.

The story has its inspiration far back in history. Jan Harold Brunvand, author of *The Vanishing Hitchhiker*, says that a prototype of the phantom hitchhiker story can be found in the Bible, in Acts 8: 26–39. The apostle Philip meets an Ethiopian eunuch, who desires to learn more about Jesus Christ. The Ethiopian picks Philip up in his chariot and takes him down to the river. After Philip baptizes the Ethiopian, "the spirit of the Lord caught away Philip, that the eunuch saw him no more." Stories of drivers who pick up hitchhikers in their horse-drawn wagons persisted in Europe and Asia for centuries. In the United States, the story acquired the automobile motif by the time of the Great Depression, giving birth to a number of variants. The story of the Swamp Girl has been passed down in Columbia for decades because it conveys the sad truth that you can't go home again.

Ghostly Mill Workers at the South Carolina State Museum

Columbia Mills was the world's first totally electric textile mill. It was built in 1894 on the eastern shore of the Congaree River because of the existence of a suitable canal that could be used to turn the turbines and generate electricity. Housing for mill workers was constructed on the west side of Congaree River. Eventually, a wooden bridge was built to transport workers to the mill. The workers' village was originally called Brookland because of the area's large number of brooks, but the name was changed to West Columbia in 1936.

In the late 1980s, the old mill building was remodeled to house the South Carolina State Museum. The museum officially opened on October 19, 1988. Today, between fifteen thousand and twenty thousand people come from all fifty states and thirty-nine foreign countries to view the exhibits in what is the largest museum in South Carolina. The South Carolina State Museum is also the only museum in the state that has the ghost of a textile worker.

After the Civil War, textile mills were viewed by many Southerners as their opportunity to join the Industrial Revolution. By the end of the nineteenth century, such mills had sprung up all over the South. One-third of the 100,000 people who worked in textile mills lived in South Carolina. Between 1880 and 1910, 25 percent of the mills' work force was under sixteen years old. Not only were the living quarters in many mill villages deplorable, but working in the mills was fraught with danger. Many people worked between ten and twelve hours a day. Workers were engulfed in stifling heat and humidity. After a while, their lungs became coated in lint and dust, resulting in a condition known as byssinosis, or "brown lung." The spinning rooms were especially hazardous. Workers ran the risk of having their hands jerked into the machines and the skin stripped from their arms. People who were not paying attention often burned themselves on the motors in the spinning room. No one knows exactly how many people were killed or injured in Southern textile mills.

One of those accident victims may be haunting the Columbia Mills site. The ghost that wanders the fourth floor of the South

Carolina State Museum has been affectionately dubbed "Bubba" by the staff. According to museum employee Tut Underwood, Bubba was a mill worker killed in an industrial accident many years ago. He is usually sighted around the Old Country Store exhibit. Bubba also seems to like the elevator. Several years ago, two women on one of the lower floors saw a man in overalls walk into the elevator. Hoping to catch the elevator before the doors closed, the two women ran as quickly as they could. Out of breath, they managed to run inside the elevator just in time. To their surprise, no one was there. On another occasion, a woman on the first floor walked into the elevator. Inside the elevator was a man dressed in overalls. When the elevator reached the fourth floor, the man stepped out, walked down a hallway, and vanished into a wall. One Sunday morning, a museum employee named Bemo Prince was walking past the Confederate submarine *Hunley* just before the museum opened when he saw a man dressed in overalls. "I just got to see his legs and feet or boots go into the shadow," Bemo said. "I went around the other side of the schoolhouse [exhibit] because I figured I could scare him. When I got around to scare him, there was nobody around."

Each floor of the South Carolina State Museum is arranged according to a theme. The first floor houses the Lipscomb Art Gallery, where visitors can view the wide diversity of art in historic and modern South Carolina. On the second floor, visitors can learn about the natural history of South Carolina. The third floor features science and technology. On the fourth floor, where South Carolina's history is documented, visitors can view Civil War exhibits, a one-room schoolhouse, a turn-of-the-century country store, and some say, the spirit of a worker from the Columbia Mills.

Cool Springs Plantation's Tippling Ghost

The name "Cool Springs" can be traced back to Sarah Nesbit's original 1767 land grant near Camden. In 1832, a planter and lawyer named John Boykin tore down the existing house on the site and built a two-story Greek Revival antebellum mansion as a summer residence and a retreat from the fever season. In the 1850s, the

Cureton family purchased the mansion and hired architect Ruben Hamilton to turn the house into one of the showcases of the entire state. Hamilton moved the chimneys to the exterior walls and added a tiered portico, rectangular additions to the east façade, and several verandas, supported by sixty-four Doric columns. Years later, two horse stables and a riding ring were added. In the 1980s, this magnificent old home, which is listed in the National Register of Historic Places, was purchased by John Bonner, retired curator of the rare book collection at the University of Georgia, and Gaffney Blalock, a professor of diagnostic medicine at Clemson University. At the time that John and Gaffney signed the contract, they did not realize that a ghost came with the old house.

In her book *South Carolina Ghosts,* author Nancy Roberts says that the ghost of a distinguished-looking, gray-haired man wearing dark trousers and a sportcoat has been seen at the house. He made his first appearance shortly after John and Gaffney had finished renovating their new home. During a dinner party the men threw to celebrate the completion of the remodeling, one of the guests went up to John and asked him who the man wearing the ascot and blazer was. John set his wineglass down near a pillar and accompanied the guest inside the old mansion in search of the uninvited guest. When John came back from his fruitless search, he returned to the place where he had set down his wineglass and was surprised to find the glass empty. John and the guest went back inside the house and made their way to the study, where recorded music was playing. Suddenly, the music stopped, and a song from a much earlier era started playing.

John contacted a friend who was familiar with the history of Cool Springs Plantation and described the spirit that his guest had seen. John's friend said that the ghost sounded like the spirit of a former owner of the plantation, Dixie Boykin, a very convivial man who enjoyed entertaining in his lavish mansion. Boykin died of a heart attack years before while inside the house. His daughter blamed her stepmother for Dixie's death because she refused to come to her father's aid when the girl told her that her father was sick.

John Bonner and Gaffney Blalock have continued the tradition of hosting lively parties at the old mansion. Music and laughter still resonate through the halls, just as they did in the nineteenth century. Residents of Camden consider themselves fortunate to have been invited to one these lavish affairs. John and Gaffney agree that their most interesting visitor never appears on the guest list.

Columbia's Horseman in the Sky

Wade Hampton III was born in Charleston on March 28, 1818. The eldest son of one of the most affluent planters in the South, Hampton grew up on the family estates at Cashier's Valley and Millwood, where he entertained himself by riding horses and hunting bears. After earning a law degree at South Carolina College in 1836, Hampton returned to the family plantations, where he lived the life of a gentleman farmer. In the 1850s, Hampton turned his attention to politics. He served in the state legislature representing Richland County from 1852 to 1856. In 1858, Hampton was elected to the state senate. After receiving a colonel's commission from the governor in 1858, Hampton resigned from the senate at the onset of the Civil War and raised a legion of artillery, infantry, and cavalry, which he outfitted with his own money.

Despite the fact that he had little military experience, Hampton was a superb horseman and a natural leader. He distinguished himself in some of the bloodiest battles of the war, including Fredericksburg, Chancellorsville, Brandy Station, and Gettysburg. He was eventually promoted to lieutenant general in 1865, the only officer besides Nathan Bedford Forrest to achieve this rank in the Confederate cavalry. Following the Civil War, Hampton served as governor from 1876 to 1879 and as a U.S. senator from 1879 to 1891. In 1893, President Grover Cleveland appointed Hampton to the position of United States Railroad Commissioner. He served in this role until 1897.

By the end of his life, Wade Hampton had become one of the most beloved heroes of the Confederate cause. When his house burned down in 1899, Hampton's friends pooled their resources and built him a new house, despite his protests. After his death in Columbia on April 11, 1902, statues were erected in Hampton's honor in the South Carolina State House and the United States Capitol. In 1906, an equestrian statue of Hampton was placed on the grounds of the State House. Legend has it that Hampton himself returned to the city that honored him twelve years after his death.

In the spring of 1914, people standing at the corner of Bull and Blanding streets stared in awe at the sudden appearance of a man on horseback hovering in the sky just above the oak trees. Eyewitnesses said that the apparition was so clear that they could make out every feature, including his saddle and reins. Before long, a crowd of astonished onlookers gathered on the street corner, pointing at the phantom horseman. After a few minutes, the horse reared up and galloped up into the clouds. The next day, a crowd gathered at the same location, anxiously awaiting the reappearance of the ghostly figure. They did not have to wait long before the horseman reappeared, just above the oak trees. This was his last visit to Columbia.

After the phantom horseman's final appearance, people began speculating as to his true identity. Some people said that it was one of the Four Horsemen of the Apocalypse. Others said that it was the ghost of Wade Hampton III, whose return was most likely an omen of some sort. Today, many people believe that the spirit of Wade Hampton returned to Columbia to warn its citizens of the impending World War I, which would bring misery and heartache to the people of South Carolina, just as the Civil War had.

Charleston

THE FIRST INHABITANTS OF CHARLESTON WERE WANDO, SEWANEE, AND Kiawah Indians, who lived in the area until the mid-1700s. The first colonists from England called the city Charles Towne after their king, Charles II. Because Charleston tolerated the French Huguenots and Jews, a large number of churches were established there, earning it the name "the Holy City." In the early years, Charleston prospered as a result of the export of indigo and rice and the trade of deerskins with the Indians. During the Revolutionary War, Charlestonians protested the Tea Act of 1773 by confiscating tea and storing it in the Exchange and Custom House. In 1780, General Benjamin Lincoln surrendered his entire force of 5,400 men to the British, making the Siege of Charleston the greatest American defeat of the entire war. After the British relinquished control of the city in December 1782, its name was officially changed to Charleston.

On January 12, 1861, the Civil War began after shore batteries under the command of General Pierre Gustave Toutant Beauregard began firing on Fort Sumter. Union troops took control of Charleston in 1864. The city's postwar economic recovery was initiated by the construction of the naval yard and fertilizer plant. On August 31, 1886, a massive earthquake damaged two thousand city buildings. Amazingly, a number of Charleston's historic buildings remain intact to this day, despite the wars, hurricanes, and fires that have threatened to wipe the city off the map.

The Mournful Ghost of St. Philip's Graveyard

St. Philip's Church was the first Anglican church organized in the South. The first St. Philip's was built at the corner of Meeting and Broad streets between 1680 and 1681. After that church was damaged by a hurricane, it was replaced by a new brick building at Second Church Street in 1723. In 1835, Second St. Philip's Church burned to the ground; it was rebuilt between 1835 and 1838 and today is generally regarded as one of the most beautiful churches in America. Because St. Philip's Graveyard escaped the destruction of the first two churches, it is much older than the church that bears its name. Actually, St. Philip's Graveyard is two graveyards. The graveyard on the left of Church Street was established in 1768 for "strangers." A number of famous citizens of Charleston are buried there, including vice president and U.S. congressman John C. Calhoun, who was born upstate. The graveyard adjacent to the church, the "right" graveyard, was established in 1680 for parishioners who were "born here." People interested in the paranormal are drawn to the "right" graveyard because of the grave of a young woman named Sue Howard Hardy.

On June 10, 1987, a resident of Charleston named Harry Reynolds drove up to St. Philip's Graveyard with the intention of trying out a new camera he had purchased. Unfortunately, the graveyard was closed by the time he arrived, so he stuck his camera through the bars and took an entire roll of photographs. After the film was developed, Harry was amazed by a shot he had taken of a back row of graves. Kneeling on one of the graves in a mournful pose was the transparent image of woman.

Harry was certain that no one was in the graveyard at the time he took the picture, so he sent the photograph off to the Kodak lab where the film had been developed for analysis. Kodak's technicians determined that the photo was not a double exposure and that it had not been altered in any way. Harry then set about to identify the woman in his bizarre photograph. When he returned to

St. Philip's Graveyard, he found that the grave in his picture was that of a twenty-nine-year-old woman who had bled to death internally on June 16, 1888, six days after giving birth to a stillborn baby. The hair rose on the back of Harry's neck when it dawned upon him that the infant had died on June 10, 1888, the same day ninety-nine years before Harry took the photograph.

Ghosts of the Provost Dungeon

Charleston's Old Exchange Building is one of the most historically important colonial buildings still standing in the United States. Built in 1771 at 122 East Bay Street on the site of the Court of the Guard, the building's Great Hall hosted colonists protesting the Tea Act of 1773. On the steps of the Exchange, South Carolina declared independence from Great Britain on March 28, 1776.

Beneath this elegant building, however, is one of the most dismal prisons in the country. Known as the Provost Dungeon, it was constructed with barrel-vaulted ceilings that are only one brick thick at the point of the vault. The ceilings and columns also support the upper floors of the Old Exchange. Countless loads of sand were used to support the original purbeck stone of the main floor. The Provost Dungeon may have been an architectural wonder, but it was totally unsuited for human occupation. Not only was it cold and damp, but rats scampered freely among the prisoners, spreading disease. Sick prisoners were housed with healthy ones, and everyone ate contaminated food and breathed stale air. Many prisoners were shackled to the walls.

The most famous prisoners were patriots arrested by Lord Cornwallis after the British captured Charleston in 1780. On August 27, 1780, thirty-eight prominent citizens, including Thomas Heyward Jr., Edward Rutledge, and Governor Christopher Gadsden, were imprisoned there until they were sent to St. Augustine, Florida. All of these upstanding citizens, including two young women from prominent families, were forced to share space with thieves, murderers, prostitutes, and deserters. Twenty-three other patriots underwent the same horrible experience in the Provost Dungeon when they were arrested on November 15, 1780. It is small wonder that the old dungeon is haunted by the spirits of the men and women who suffered and died there.

The Provost Dungeon was restored in 1966. A number of important discoveries were made during the restoration, including a section of the Half Moon Bastion, which was once part of the original foundation of Charles Town. People interested in the paranormal believe that changes made in the original structure might have awakened the ghosts that now mingle with the tourists as they walk through the dungeon.

The spirits in the Provost Dungeon seem to be most active on dark and gloomy days. Sometimes, when no groups of tourists have been passing through the dungeon, tour guides walking past the remains of Half Moon Bastion have noticed chains stretched across the entrance swinging by themselves in unison. On one occasion, a chain across the doorway fell on the floor, frightening one of the tour guides half out of her wits. Lights suspended from the ceiling have also been known to swing in empty parts of the dungeon. Tourists have reported hearing cries and moans emanating from the dark recesses of the dungeon. Women are particularly uncomfortable in the Provost Dungeon. One female tourist reported being pushed against the wall. Another woman felt as if she was being strangled by invisible hands.

No prisoners have been held in the Provost Dungeon since 1782. Today, it is occupied by mannequins designed by local historian Emmett Robinson. The plastic figures depict men and women who were incarcerated here as war prisoners in 1780, as well as several unsavory individuals. If the testimony of eyewitnesses can be believed, the mannequins are not the only remnants of Charleston's colonial history that are still trapped inside the dank prison walls.

Second Act at the Dock Street Theater

The Dock Street Theater was the first building in America designed solely for theatrical performances. The theater opened at the corner of Church and Dock streets on February 12, 1735, with the production of a bawdy farce by George Farquhar titled *The Recruiting Officer*. In 1740, the theater was destroyed by a fire that also consumed most of Charleston's historic French Quarter. In 1809, a new building, the Planter's Hotel, was constructed on the site of the old theater. For more than fifty years, the Planter's Hotel hosted scores of plantation owners and merchants eager to spend an evening drinking, playing cards, and dallying with the prostitutes who earned their living there.

After the Civil War, the structure fell into disrepair. The old building received a new lease on life in 1935, when it was renovated by the Works Progress Administration. Under the supervision of architect Alfred Simons, the Dock Street Theater has been embellished with beautiful woodwork carved from native cypress. Today, the theater's checkered past has helped make it one of the most photographed sites in the entire city. According to local lore, two figures from the theater's storied past are still roaming its shadowy hallways and darkened rooms.

Many locals believe that the Dock Street Theater is haunted by the spirit of one of the Planter's Hotel's most famous patrons, nineteenth-century actor Junius Brutus Booth. In the years immediately preceding the Civil War, Booth was known as the greatest actor of his day. Today, he is remembered primarily as the father of Edwin and John Wilkes Booth. Eyewitnesses describe his spirit as five foot seven and wearing a top hat, a frock coat, and knee boots.

The Dock Street Theater is also said to be haunted by a female ghost who is seen on the second floor. She is allegedly the spirit of a prostitute named Nettie Dickerson, who used her charms to make a living from the attentions of the men who patronized the Planter's Hotel in the 1830s. According to Edward B. Macy and Julian T. Buxton III, the authors of *The Ghosts of Charleston*, Nettie secured employment in the office of St. Philip's Church when she arrived in Charleston in 1838. Before long, though, she became restless in the boring confines of the church. She longed to be a part of the thriving social scene that focused around the Planter's Hotel. In 1839, Nettie strode into the lobby wearing a revealing red dress, and she immediately attracted the attention of every man present. She soon became one of the most popular prostitutes working out of the Planter's Hotel. Despite that fact that she had a beautiful wardrobe, handsome lovers, and plenty of money, she harbored a secret desire to return to St. Philip's Church. One evening, as storm clouds rolled across the night sky, she was standing on the second floor balcony, staring wistfully at the steeple of St. Philip's, when she was struck by lightning. In that brief instant, Nettie's dream of redemption was obliterated. In another much less dramatic version of the story, Nettie was the victim of a botched abortion.

Like many individuals for whom death was sudden and unexpected, Nettie Dickerson's ghost is a restless spirit. For many years, the translucent figure of a red-headed woman in a red dress has been seen walking down the hallways and staircases on the theater's second floor. Her shimmering form passes through walls in a seemingly wide-eyed trance. In many of these eyewitness accounts, Nettie's ghost is portrayed as walking down the hall on her knees. Her strange appearance can be explained by the fact that during renovations in 1936, the WPA workers raised the floor on the second story by more than a foot. Totally unaware of the structural change that was made to the second floor, Nettie's ghost continues to walk the halls just as she did in the 1830s and 1840s.

The Dock Street Theater has presented more than 150 productions since it opened in 1937. More than one million people have experienced the thrill of watching first-rate actors apply their craft in such classics of the theater as *A Streetcar Named Desire*. However, some patrons claim that the most exciting performances at the Dock Street Theater are the random appearances of its resident ghosts.

Restless Wraiths of the Old Charleston Jail

The Old Charleston Jail stands on the site of a building that dated back to 1738 and served as a slave workhouse, a poorhouse, and a hospital for vagrants and other impoverished people. In 1802, the old building was replaced with the present structure. Pirates were incarcerated here in the 1820s while awaiting execution. In 1822, a fireproof wing, designed by Robert Mills, was added. The building was renovated again in 1855, when an octagonal wing replaced Mills's fireproof wing. During the Civil War, Confederate and Federal soldiers were held prisoner at the Old Charleston Jail. Some of the Union prisoners were black soldiers who had fought with the 54th Massachusetts. In 1886, the top floor and tower were removed after being damaged by an earthquake. Prisoners continued to be held in the Old Charleston Jail until it was finally closed in 1939. The old building remained vacant until 2000, when it was stabilized before being completely revamped as a part of the campus for the American College for the Building Arts.

The Old Charleston Jail's haunted reputation is based largely on the fact that so many people suffered there. The jail was designed to hold 128 prisoners, but it was not unusual for more than three hundred people to be held there at any one time. Under these extremely cramped conditions, disease ran rampant. Prisoners also had to face the likelihood of being raped or attacked while serving their sentence in the Old Charleston Jail. The most unruly criminals were starved, shackled, and tortured. By the time the prison closed, approximately ten thousand people had died there.

The most notorious prisoners in the Old Charleston Jail were Lavinia and John Fisher. In 1819, the couple ran an inn known as the "Six Mile House." The story goes that a man named John Peeples had left Georgia in a horse-drawn wagon and was on his way to Charleston late one evening when he decided to spend the night at the Fishers' inn. Lavinia, a strikingly beautiful woman, offered him a glass of tea, which he accepted but did not drink. He became nervous when the couple asked him how much money he had with him, so when he retired to his room for the night, he slept in a chair by the door instead of in the bed. Suddenly, he was awakened in the middle of the night by a strange sound. Wiping the sleep from his eyes, Peeples stared in awe as the bed disappeared through a hole that had opened up in the floor. A faint beam of light in the room illuminated a grisly pile of bones inside the hole. Panic-stricken, Peeples jumped through an open window and rode off into the night.

The next morning, Peeples told his story to the authorities in Charleston. The sheriff's deputy and a group of deputized citizens rushed to the Six Mile House, where they found the bone pit under the bed in the room where Peeples had stayed. The tea the couple had offered Peeples was found to contain an herb that would have put him into a deep sleep for several hours. John and Lavinia Fisher were immediately arrested, along with five accomplices, and placed in the Old Charleston Jail. Following a swift trial, John and the other men were found guilty. After her husband was hanged, Lavinia appeared before the court in a flattering white wedding gown in the hope that her beauty would convince the court to spare her life. Fearing retribution from the hundreds of people who had gathered around the courthouse, the judges found Lavinia guilty and sentenced her to be hanged. The story goes that as she stood upon the gallows erected on Meeting Street, Lavinia cried, "If any of you have something to tell the Devil, tell me now because I'm about to see him."

The story of the woman known today as the nation's first female serial killer did not end with her execution. Her ghost has been seen hovering around her grave in the Unitarian Cemetery. Lavinia's spirit is also said to be an active presence in the Old Charleston Jail. Visitors' jewelry other personal possessions, such as rings and handkerchiefs, are occasionally "spirited away" by an unseen hand. Some people claim to have been pushed by some sort of invisible force. Other weird occurrences that cannot be directly attributed to Lavinia have also taken place in the Old Charleston Jail. Cold spots have been detected in the jail during hot summer days. Cell-phone conversations are occasionally disrupted. Tourists have captured numerous orbs and EVPs while touring the old jail. Some employees and tourists have experienced shortness of breath on the main staircase.

The Old Charleston Jail's resemblance to a medieval castle is fitting considering the pain and suffering that thousands of prisoners endured within its walls for more than a century. The paranormal activity witnessed by hundreds of people over the years suggests that some of the anguish of the former tenants may have been absorbed into the very fabric of the old jail. It is also possible that the spirits trapped inside the Old Charleston Jail continue to make their presence known so that their inhumane treatment will never be forgotten.

The Thwarted Lovers of Fenwick Hall Plantation

After John Fenwick arrived on John's Island in 1703, he was appointed commissioner of the Indian Tract. He married Elizabeth Gibbes, the daughter of Governor Robert Gibbes, and moved into a house made of notched logs on the Stono River. In 1730, the log cabin was replaced with a beautiful Georgian-style plantation house, known as Fenwick Hall. After John's son, Edward, inherited the eleven thousand-acre estate in 1747, he added two-story brick extensions at the sides of the mansion. Edward was an avid horse breeder who built stables and a three-mile racetrack on the property. Known today as the "Founder of the Turf in Carolina," Edward was one of the eight founders of the original South Carolina Jockey Club. In 1779, Edward's sons, Edward Jr. and Thomas, joined the British forces that took over Fenwick Hall.

After the Revolutionary War, Thomas fled to Jamaica, and Edward Jr. moved to Edisto, where he set up a horse-breeding farm. Fenwick Hall Plantation passed into the hands of Gibbes family, who retained ownership of the property until John Gibbes died in 1803. The house was used as a hospital by both Confederate and Union forces during the Civil War, and a number of different people owned Fenwick Hall Plantation in the nineteenth and twentieth centuries. In the 1930s, Victor Morawetz of New York bought Fenwick Hall and repaired the dilapidated old house. In 1980, Fenwick Hall Hospital, a private alcohol and drug abuse treatment center, was housed in the old mansion. The City of Charleston annexed Fenwick Hall Hospital in 1980 and zoned the former plantation grounds for development. After Fenwick Hospital closed in 1995, the mansion was purchased by private individuals, who made extensive renovations to it. Today, the private residence has had much of its former grandeur restored. Even two of the mansion's ghosts are still there.

The ghost story of Fenwick Hall takes place in the mid-eighteenth century. In the version of the story told by Margaret Rhett Martin in *Charleston Ghosts*, Edward Fenwick Sr. had a teenage daughter, Ann, who loved to go horse riding. One day, Edward, who doted on the girl, gave her a beautiful black stallion as a present. Ann rode the beautiful thoroughbred every day and immediately bonded with the horse. Over time, she also became very close to Tony, the handsome groom who often accompanied her on her rides. Within a few months, Ann fell deeply in love with the young man. One day, she walked into her father's study and, in a soft, trembling voice, told him that she loved Tony and wanted to marry him. Edward rose from his chair and, in an angry voice, told his daughter that she could not marry Tony because he was not worthy of her. Several weeks later, she again asked her father's permission to marry Tony, but Edward Sr. was still adamantly opposed to the union. In desperation, the love-struck girl decided to elope with Tony. On a designated night, the couple walked to the marshes of the Ashley River in hope of finding a boat. When no boat could be found, Ann and Tony were forced to spend the night in an abandoned cabin.

Ann and Tony were awakened the next morning by loud knocking at the door. Standing in the doorway were Edward Sr. and several other men. When Ann informed her father that she and Tony had been married the day before, he ordered his men to place Tony on a horse, with a noose around his neck and the rope tied to a tree branch. Ann's father then placed a riding whip in her hand and commanded her to strike the horse on the rump. With tears in her eyes, the girl did as she was told. She then screamed "Tony!" and collapsed on the ground. Ann was taken to her room and laid on the bed. When she awoke, she began searching through the house for Tony, even though her mother told her that the groom was dead. For the rest of her life, Ann sat in the east parlor or wandered through the rooms of Fenwick Hall, asking, "Tony! Tony! Tony! Where are you?" For more than two hundred years, occupants of Fenwick Hall have heard ghostly footsteps walking down the hallways and a plaintive voice crying, "Tony! Tony! Tony!"

In a second version of the tale, Tony himself haunts Fenwick Hall Plantation. According to some people, Tony's body was jerked so violently off his horse that the noose ripped off his head. For years, his headless corpse has been riding through marshes, searching for his lost love, or, perhaps, for his head. Many residents of John's Island claim to have seen the headless horseman of Fenwick Hall on moonlit nights.

In 2001, developers began construction of several hundred housing units on the plantation property. Today, townhomes and condos are plainly visible through the trees that line the 55-acre estate. Fenwick Hall Plantation's rural ambiance may be gone forever, but the tragically romantic legend of Ann Fenwick's illicit love for her groom is likely to persist for years to come.

The Regretful Wraith of Sword Gates House

The stately old manor known today as the Sword Gates House was built in 1776 as a school for the daughters of the upper-class families of Charleston. For fifty years, the school was bordered only by a hedge and a wooden gate. The strict headmistress, Madame Talvande, was convinced that her school was amply fortified to prevent her girls from absconding during the night. In 1828, however, the pampered, headstrong daughter of a wealthy planter destroyed Madame Talvande's confidence in the school's security system and in her own ability to protect her students.

Fifteen-year-old Maria Whately was born to a life of privilege on Pine Baron Plantation on Edisto Island. The strikingly beautiful girl had already caught the eye of a number of smitten young men when she met George Morris and immediately fell in love. Maria's father, Colonel Whately, disapproved of the match. While it was true that Morris made a good living, his earnings did not come close to matching the annual income of one of the wealthiest families in Charleston. And, to make matters worse, he was from New York, an outsider. Morris, on the other hand, was determined to make Maria his wife. Colonel Whately tried to discourage Morris from courting his daughter by convincing his friends on Edisto Island to close their doors to him. Undeterred, Morris pitched a tent a short distance from Pine Baron Plantation and continued to see Maria.

The Whatelys had intended to educate Maria at home. However, Maria's stubborn refusal to stop seeing George Morris compelled her parents to send their daughter to Madame Talvande's girls' school at 39 Legare Street, where young women were taught to be young ladies. Maria obeyed her parents and went to Madame Talvande's school, but she was miserable without George. Her situation would have been intolerable if George had not promised to marry her as soon as possible. After a few seemingly endless months, she received a message from George that they would be married on March 8, 1828. George's friend, Mrs. Blank, would arrange for Maria's arrival at St. Michael's Church. That night, George huddled in the cold and damp, anxiously awaiting the arrival of his beloved. Finally, a carriage pulled up at the church. Inside the carriage were Mrs. Blank, Maria, and a bridesmaid, Sarah Seabrook. After the minister, Mr. Dalcho, pronounced the couple man and wife, Mrs. Blank told Maria that she had to return to school that night but added that she could leave the next morning for her honeymoon.

After the carriage dropped Maria off at the school, the young bride tried to sneak through the front door, but her foot slipped on the wet pavement, and she fell in the mud. When the woman in charge of the girls' dormitory, Miss Halburn, saw Maria standing on the front stoop in her muddy wet dress, she was so afraid that the girl would catch cold that she neglected to ask her where she had been. Maria went directly to her room and packed her trousseau. The next morning, George Morris appeared at the front door of the school and told the housekeeper that he had come to pick up Mrs. Morris. Madame Talvande stepped in front of the housekeeper and informed him that there was no Mrs. Morris in her school. The tittering of the girls standing behind her suggested to Madame Talvande that there might indeed be a Mrs. Morris among them. She told George that she would look into the matter and shut the door. Madame Talvande then ordered all of the students and staff to parade onto the front lawn. Standing ramrod straight, she asked if a Mrs. Morris was present. After a few moments, Maria took a few hesitating steps forward and curtsied in front of the head mistress. With her eyes cast to the ground, Maria admitted that she had married George Morris the night before at St. Michael's Church. Madame Talvande was speechless for a few seconds. Then she flew into a rage, berating Maria, Miss Halburn, and all the other members of the staff. As soon as Madame Talvande's back was turned, George took Maria by the arm and whisked her away in his carriage.

Maria and George had, by all accounts, a happy life following her escape from Madame Talvande's school. Her father eventually forgave his errant daughter and saw to it that she was well provided for. The same cannot be said for Madame Talvande, however. Concerned that the reputation of her school would suffer from the bad publicity, she had a high wall constructed around the garden. The wall had wooden gates until Madame Talvande purchased a pair of elaborate wrought-iron gates for the entranceway of the school in 1838, giving the house its present name. For the next eleven years, there were no elopements from her school, but the trust that the parents had in her to protect their daughters gradually eroded. The school closed in 1849 and became a private residence.

For years, subsequent owners of the old school have seen the rueful ghost of the headmistress. They have said that her ghost enters the north bedroom upstairs and vanishes after a few seconds. Sometimes, as the doorknob to the stateroom slowly turns, nothing but a cool breeze of air enters the room. She often appears as a full-body apparition in the stateroom, dressed in the severe fashions of the early nineteenth century. Her eyes scan the room, looking for miscreant girls. Madame Talvande's ghost has also been seen on the top-floor piazza, gazing over the grounds of the former campus.

Since the closing of Madame Talvande's school for girls, the Sword Gates House has served as a private residence and a bed-and-breakfast. The only constant inside the house seems to be the vigilant spirit of the former headmistress, who continues to make sure that none of her charges runs away as Maria Whaley did long ago.

The Citadel's Lost Cadet

Charleston's Embassy Suites Hotel is unique in that it is housed inside a local landmark. The structure on this site was originally a fort built in 1758 to protect the city. Charleston sold the fort to the State of South Carolina in 1789. The building was used as a warehouse to store and inspect tobacco until 1822, when the state decided to build a new fort on the site. Four years later, construction of a new fort, "The Citadel," was complete. The Citadel was converted into a military school in 1842. In the 1850s, a third story and east and west wings were added to the building. Federal troops were barracked in the Citadel during the Civil War. Before leaving the city, the Yankees burned the west wing, which was not rebuilt until 1882, when the Citadel Military College opened its doors once again. The military school continued to operate at the site until 1922, when it moved to its current campus on the banks of the Ashley River.

In 1996, the original Citadel was renovated as an upscale hotel. In its new incarnation, the Embassy Suites Hotel has 153 guest rooms, nine meeting rooms, a ballroom, a spacious courtyard, and a five-story atrium with a twelve-foot fountain. For those guests who like a good scare, the hotel is also said to offer a very gruesome-looking ghost.

The spirit that haunts the Embassy Suites is known as "the Lost Cadet." Witnesses describe the entity as a teenager, dressed in the nineteenth-century Citadel cadet's uniform. Oddly enough, he is smiling, even though the upper half of his head is missing from the eyebrows on up. Employees, who call this frightful apparition

"Half-head," say that the severe trauma to the cadet's head seems to have been caused by a cannonball. The manifestations of this maimed wraith are so disturbing that some maids are reluctant to enter several of the rooms.

Guests have also made the acquaintance of the Lost Cadet. In the early 2000s, a cardiologist flew into Charleston for a conference. When she arrived at the Embassy Suites, she checked in and went straight to Room 113. At 8:30 the next morning, she was making a pot of coffee when she turned around and saw a young man who was staring straight at her. He was wearing a gray coat with a dark gray stripe down the back. Even more disturbing than the sudden appearance of a man in her room was the fact that the top of his skull, from the eyebrows up, was completely missing. She was so unnerved that she dropped the coffee she was holding and ran screaming to the front desk. The clerk asked her what she had seen, but she just shook her head and wept. The woman checked out and refused to come back to the building.

In spite of the extensive changes that have been made to the hotel, it still has a very forbidding look to it, at least from the outside. With its parapets and turrets still intact, the building bears a closer resemblance to a medieval castle than to a four-star hotel. The periodic appearances of the Lost Cadet are another reminder of the hotel's violent past.

Garden Street Theater Ghosts

The Garden Street Theater is a remnant of a bygone era. When the theater opened on January 14, 1918, patrons eager to view vaudeville acts and the latest silent movies paraded past an assortment of hanging baskets, trellises, and caged canaries. Musical accompaniment was provided by a specialized organ called a "fotophone," which could produce amazing sound effects, such as the creaking of a door and the firing of a pistol. Stage shows as well as movies were shown at the Garden after the nearby Victory Theater was razed in 1946. The theater continued to offer movies and stage shows throughout the 1950s. Schools, churches, and various other organizations, including the College of Charleston and the Charleston Opera Company, used the Garden Theater in the 1960s. The theater was closed in the 1970s before undergoing extensive remodeling when the City of Charleston leased it in 1977. One year later, the 650-seat theater reopened with movies and stage shows.

In the 1980s, the Garden Theater was transformed into a performing arts space. In 2002, the City of Charleston decided not to renew its lease, so the theater was sold to a group of private investors. In 2003, the decision was made to convert the Garden into a retail store. In 2004, the seats, curtains and rigging were donated to an opera company in Pennsylvania. At the time of this writing, the only original parts of the theater that remain are the façade, the interior detail, and sad memories of Charleston's segregated past.

In the 1980s and 1990s, rumors spread that the Garden Theater was haunted. Janitors refused to work alone or at night. The balcony, they said, was the scariest part of the theater. The most famous sighting at the theater occurred late one evening in the summer of 1994. A janitor was about to turn the breakers on when he saw a man sitting in the fourth row. The man appeared to be an African-American male in his sixties or seventies. The janitor walked down to the fifth row, shined his flashlight in the man's face, and asked him what he was doing there. The man immediately stood up and ran to the back of the theater. Two weeks later, the janitor saw the same intruder; this time, the man was sitting in the front row. The janitor walked behind the seat where the man was sitting and informed him that he was trespassing on private property. When the man turned around, his eyes were bloodshot. Sweat trickled down his face. The janitor was so shaken that he dropped his flashlight and left. He refused to return to work, despite the entreaties of the manager.

The ghost's strange behavior can be explained by the fact that until the 1970s, African-American patrons were restricted to the balcony, which was hotter in the summer than any other part of the theater. Quite possibly, the spirit of the black man was reveling in his freedom to sit in the lower level of the theater late at night, when he was the only one present.

Female Revenants of the Unitarian Church Cemetery

The Unitarian Church in Charleston is the second oldest church on the city peninsula. In 1772, the Society of Dissenters decided that their building on Meeting Street was not large enough to accommodate the church's increasing size, so plans were made for the construction of another church on Archdale Street to handle the "overflow." The new church was not formally dedicated until 1787 because American and British troops used the church for a barracks throughout the Revolutionary War. The two churches did not become two separate entities until 1817, when one of the ministers, Anthony Forster, and a number of members of the Society of Dissenters decided to become Unitarians. More than half of the congregation moved with their minister to the Archdale Street church, which was renamed "The Second Independent Church in Charleston." The name of the church was changed again in 1839, when it was rechartered as the Unitarian Church. Since then, the Unitarian Church has narrowly escaped total destruction several times. The Great Charleston Fire of 1861 burned the fence enclosing the church but left the building untouched. The Charleston Earthquake of 1886 toppled the steeple, but the church itself was left intact. When Hurricane Hugo blew into Charleston in 1989, it spared the church but felled several old trees, which damaged a number of tombstones in the churchyard. Like the church itself, the resilient spirits of several women interred in the adjacent graveyard seem to have been unfazed by the passing of time.

One of the ghosts who haunts the Unitarian Church graveyard is said to be the spirit of Mary Whitridge, who lived in Mount Pleasant around the turn of the century. In 1906, her husband Edward was stricken with what he believed to be tuberculosis, or "consumption," as it was known at the time. On the advice of his wife, Edward decided to travel by ship to Baltimore, where he planned to consult with a physician at Johns Hopkins. His ship left Charleston harbor on January 11, 1907. Unbeknownst to Mary or his doctor, Edward was actually too ill to complete the journey, and he died en route. Upon the ship's arrival in Baltimore, Edward's body was taken to the city morgue, where the coroner determined that he had died of heart failure. His corpse was interred in the city cemetery.

Coincidentally, Mary passed away on the same day Edward died. It turned out that Mary, who was sixty-one, also had a weak heart that finally gave out on July 13, 1906. She was buried in the Unitarian churchyard. Next to her grave is an empty plot where Edward was to be buried. Today, Mary Whitridge's bright, shimmering spirit allegedly floats around the graveyard where she and Edward enjoyed taking walks in happier days. Witnesses sense that she is a melancholy spirit who is looking for something or someone—quite possibly her husband, whose corpse was not united with her in the Unitarian Church graveyard.

A notorious female spirit also walks among the tombstones at the graveyard. This is said to be the ghost of Lavinia Fisher, who is often referred to as America's first female serial killer. She was an extraordinarily beautiful woman who, with her husband, John, managed a hotel—the Six Mile House—in the Charleston Neck region between 1810 and 1820. The Fishers were said to murder their guests in their beds and steal their possessions. The couple sold their victims' horses and carriages at auction and pocketed the proceeds. John and Lavinia were hanged on February 18, 1820. Lavinia was wearing her white wedding dress at the time. She was buried in an unmarked grave in the Unitarian cemetery, the only cemetery that would take her body. For many years, visitors to the graveyard have seen the apparition of a woman wearing a white wedding dress wandering through the cemetery. Supposedly, she is looking for the judge who sentenced her to hang. Ironically, he too is buried in the Unitarian churchyard. Until the Unitarian Church began locking the gates to the graveyard at night, it was not uncommon for large groups of people taking tours through the city to see the ghost of Lavinia Fisher.

The third spirit in the Unitarian churchyard is the subject of one of Charleston's most intriguing legends. She is said to be the ghost of a fourteen-year-old girl, Anna Ravenel. Her father, Edmund Ravenel, was a noted conchologist and professor at the local medical college. Dr. Ravenel, who kept a house on Sullivan's Island, also practiced medicine there. In 1827, he befriended a young soldier, Private Edgar A. Perry, who was stationed at Fort Moultrie on the tip of Sullivan's Island. According to the legend, Anna Ravenel and

Edgar Perry fell in love. When Dr. Ravenel discovered that his daughter's boyfriend was a soldier who was far beneath her, he closed his house on Sullivan's Island and returned to Charleston. Edgar's passion was so strong that he followed Anna to Charleston and rendezvoused with her in the Unitarian Church Cemetery. When Dr. Ravenel discovered that Anna's lover was pursuing her in Charleston, he locked her in her room and forbade her to leave. During her confinement in her room, Anna kept her spirits up by writing letters to Edgar, but her health began to decline. Several months after Dr. Ravenel locked Anna in her room, she died of yellow fever.

Edgar Perry did not immediately learn about Anna's illness because he had been transferred away from Fort Moultrie. He returned to Charleston as soon as he learned of Anna's death, but her father would not allow him to attend her funeral. To discourage Edgar from visiting Anna's grave at the Unitarian Church graveyard, all of the graves in the family plot were dug to a depth of at least three feet so they would be indistinguishable from Anna's grave.

In the legend that has been passed down from generation to generation for 150 years, the young soldier who fell in love with Anna Ravenel is Edgar Allan Poe, who used the name Edgar A. Perry when he was stationed at Fort Moultrie from 1827 to 1828. Poe not only made the acquaintance of Dr. Edmund Ravenel during his stay on Sullivan's Island, but he is also said to have modeled the narrator of "The Gold Bug" after the renowned conchologist. The more romantically inclined residents of Charleston believe that Anna Ravenel was the inspiration for Poe's poem "Annabel Lee." Anna Ravenel, they say, has joined Mary Whitridge and Lavinia Fisher in their eternal search for the men who changed their lives forever.

Poogan's Porch

Built in 1886, the building on 72 Queen Street that now houses one of Charleston's most popular restaurants was originally owned by two spinster sisters, Elizabeth and Zoe St. Amand. Both women were schoolteachers, but they had entirely different temperaments. Elizabeth, the older sister, was talkative and outgoing. Zoe, on the other hand, was a shy, proper woman who rarely spoke. She was reputed to be very strict with her students at the Craft's House

School, which stood just up the street on the corner of Queen and Legare streets. The two women lived happily together until Elizabeth died in 1945. Unable to fully recover from her sister's death, Zoe stared vacantly out her windows without acknowledging the waving hands of people passing by her house. She was also said to sleepwalk around her house at night. Zoe was confined to a mental institution in 1952 and died two years later. Zoe never returned physically to her beloved home, but, according to the owners and staff at the restaurant, her spirit has.

In 1976, Bobbie Ball purchased the St. Amand house and set about converting it into a restaurant. She had no sooner begun renovations before she made the acquaintance of a little neighborhood dog who showed up on the porch one day begging scraps of food. Bobbie and the little West Highland white terrier bonded immediately, and Poogan, as he was called, became a fixture at the new restaurant. Guests were charmed by the scruffy little dog that greeted them as they walked across the front porch. Bobbie eventually named her restaurant after Poogan, who died of natural causes in 1979.

Bobbie has remodeled Poogan's Porch several times since 1976. Some experts in the paranormal believe that the alterations Bobbie has made in the old house over the years have agitated one of the original owners. One night in the early 2000s, Bobbie was closing up the restaurant when she had difficulty setting the security codes on the burglar alarm. She telephoned the alarm company and was talking to one of the technicians when a barstool flew across the room and knocked over several other barstools. While Bobbie was picking up the stools, the heavy kitchen door slammed open. After Bobbie regained her composure, she concluded that Zoe's ghost was upset about the problems with the burglar alarm.

Zoe's presence in the restaurant has also been sensed by customers and staff. Objects sitting on tables appear to have been knocked on the floor by an unseen hand.

Waiters and waitresses have seen an old woman in a black dress walking down the hallway. The old woman always disappears when anyone approaches her. Staff members who have heard the crashing sounds of pots and pans falling on the floor have walked into the kitchen and found everything in place. One night, a waiter who was closing up for the night walked up to the second floor and noticed that all of the chairs were pulled out from the tables, as they were supposed to be. However, the tablecloth in front of one of the chairs was pushed inward, as if someone were sitting at the table. Another waiter walked into the kitchen and saw an old woman in black mixing dough in a bowl. When he told her that she was not supposed to be there, she vanished. Even guests staying on the fourth and fifth floors of the Mills Hotel across the street from Poogan's Porch have seen a woman in a black dress staring out of one the restaurant windows long after closing time. Sometimes, the woman appears to be waving at the spectators. Thinking that the woman was a customer who was accidentally locked in the restaurant, some witnesses have notified the police. No elderly woman has ever been found in the restaurant after hours.

One of the most startling encounters in Poogan's Porch took place in 1996. A couple staying in the Mills Hotel was celebrating their wedding anniversary. On the night of their anniversary, they decided to have dinner at Poogan's Porch. They were looking over the menu when the woman left to go to the restroom. She was washing her hands in the sink when she heard someone pounding frantically on the restroom door. In a loud voice the woman said, "Someone is in here!" but the pounding continued. Exasperated, she opened the door, but no one was there. Shaking her head, she returned to her place in front of the mirror and continued washing her hands. When she finished, she looked up at the mirror and saw the reflection of an old woman in a black dress standing behind her. The old woman seemed to be leering at her. Terror-stricken, the woman screamed and ran out the bathroom door. She continued running through the restaurant and out the front door. By the time her husband found her, she was huddled on the front lawn, sobbing uncontrollably.

Apparently, Poogan is haunting the restaurant as well. Guests have reported feeling something brush against their legs just above their ankles. The spectral pooch has also been sighted a couple of times running through the restaurant. The fact that the little dog lies buried in the garden might at least partially explain why he is so attached to the old place.

A number of famous people have dined at Poogan's Porch over the years, including Paul Newman and Joanne Woodward, Jodie Foster, Jim Carrey, Tennessee Williams, and James Brolin and Barbara Streisand. It is possible that the ghost of Zoe St. Amand is not impressed by the large number of famous people who have walked through the front door of her former home. The disturbances that make working and dining at Poogan's Porch a highly interesting experience could be Zoe's way of expressing her disapproval of all the strangers who have been parading through Poogan's Porch for more than three decades.

The Playful Spirit of the 1837 Bed and Breakfast

A great deal of Charleston's appeal lies in its splendid array of antebellum mansions. Before the Civil War, Charleston was the most prosperous city in the South, due in large part to the slave trade. In the late eighteenth and early nineteenth centuries, Charleston was the main point of entry for slaves sent to the United States. In fact, 70 percent of all of the slaves who were transported to America passed through Charleston harbor. One of Charleston's saddest ghost stories hearkens back to the days when countless families were torn asunder and sold at Charleston's Old Slave Market.

The 1837 Bed and Breakfast, built in 1837 by Henry Cobiah, is a stunning example of the Charleston single house. During the 1830s, a slave couple lived in a room on the third floor along with their nine-year-old son, George. In 1843, financial adversity forced Cobiah to sell several of his slaves, including George's parents. The next day, the little boy walked down to the dock and asked a man where his parents were. He was told that they had been taken aboard a ship that was currently docked in the middle of Charleston harbor. Motivated by the hope that he might be reunited with his parents, Henry stole a rowboat and rowed in the direction of his parents' ship. All at once, the little boat capsized, and George was drowned.

Jane M. Feind, the concierge at the 1837 Bed and Breakfast, believes that George remains in the old house because it is where he grew up. It is also the last place where he lived with his parents. His mischievous behavior has earned George the label of "poltergeist" among the staff at the inn. "You don't see him," Feind said. "He just makes things move. He will open doors, he rocks chairs, and he turns lights on and off. Most of [these disturbances take the form of] the mattress shaking, or lights turn on that were turned off. He gets blamed if the radio goes off in the middle of the night. And what usually happens is that someone the night before has the alarm set, and instead of turning it to 'off,' they just let the music play until the radio sets back up again. Also, if you have a soda can or something else that beads water up on it, the beads of water will walk off the glass tabletops." However, Feind believes that beads walk off the table because the house is not level, not because the ghosts are active.

Feind had an otherworldly experience in Room 4, which is where George seems to be the most active: "At the time, it was the concierge's room. The configuration going into the bathroom was different then than it is now. There were French doors that went into the bathroom. One night, I was awakened by one of the French doors just banging back and forth. I got up, walked over, and shut the doors. I went to bed and was awakened again by the French doors just banging back and forth. I sat up in bed and said, 'George! Stop it! You're scaring me!' and the doors stopped moving, so I went back to sleep. That was my experience with George."

A former concierge at the 1837 Bed and Breakfast has also been spooked in Room 4: "A couple of times when I came into the room, the TV was on, and I had turned it off. Sometimes, I'll turn the bathroom light on, and the main light acts like it's dying. I remember going to sleep one night. I went to the bathroom, and when I got back, the TV came on. At six in the morning, the TV came on. I said to myself, 'Worse case scenario, it's George.' And I went back to sleep."

On several occasions, George has surprised guests while they were asleep. Angela Creach, head housekeeper at the inn, said, "Guests have heard George enter the room and walk around. Then he shakes the bed hard and tries to wake them up. They look around, and there's nobody there." Angela felt George shake the bed one night when she was asleep in the room. "I told him to stop, and he did," Angela said.

Feind says that one of the funniest incidents at the 1837 Bed and Breakfast took place in May 2002: "We had a lady come down at breakfast, and she said, 'Did we have an earthquake last night?' And I said, 'I don't think so.' She said her bed was moving. I said, 'Was the chandelier moving too?' She said, 'No.' I said, 'Well, that's not an earthquake.' I didn't tell her about the ghost. Chances are that it was George acting up again. She asked me to call the earthquake people, and I did, and they said we didn't have an earthquake. She accused them of covering it up."

Long time employees at the 1837 Bed and Breakfast have become somewhat laissez faire about the inn's resident ghost. The disturbances in the house seem to be more characteristic of the pranks of an attention-starved child than the fiendish activity of a malevolent entity. "I think George just wants us to know he's here," Feind said.

Ghosts of the Battery Carriage House Inn

In the nineteenth century, the Battery was one of the most exclusive residential neighborhoods in Charleston. During the Civil War, however, the waterfront area was also one of the most embattled. Beginning in 1861, Federal forces under the command of Rear Admiral Samuel F. Du Pont blockaded Charleston. Because Confederate general Pierre Gustave Toutant Beauregard did not want to see the city fall to Federal gunboats as New Orleans had done, he began installing powerful defenses. To guard the harbor entrance, soldiers dug artillery positions into the White Point Gardens at the foot of East Battery.

On August 21, 1863, Brigadier General Quincy Adams Gilmore's Union forces began an artillery bombardment of the city. From a special pine-log platform constructed in the salt marsh between Morris and James islands, an eight-inch Parrott rifle, dubbed the "Swamp Angel," began firing on downtown Charleston. By the end of the war, the burned-out structures in the districts near the waterfront were silent testimony to the price Charlestonians paid for their fierce resistance to Federal forces. Some people say that the fine old mansion on 20 S. Battery Street still resonates with the horror of those tragic days.

The property on which the Battery Carriage House Inn stands was purchased on June 7, 1843, by Samuel N. Stevens, who erected a large but simple house on the site at 20 S. Battery Street. In 1859, Stevens' widow sold the house and property to John F. Blacklock for $20,000. Blacklock sold the estate to Colonel Richard Lathers in 1870. Colonel Lathers, a millionaire, was a native of Georgetown. Before the Civil War, he had toured the South, begging business-men to remain loyal to the Union. After war broke out, Lathers served with the Union. In 1869, Lathers returned to South Carolina to assist with the rebuilding of the state. Lathers transformed Stevens' comparatively modest home into a palatial mansion typi-cal of the showplaces constructed during Charleston's golden age. He built a two-story addition on the northeast corner, a ballroom over a passageway to the west, and a mansard roof to form a fourth story, which Lathers used as a library.

Lathers held gatherings at 20 S. Battery Street to bring leaders of the South together with those of the North. In 1873, Lathers invited the former governor of New York, Horatio Seymour, and the editor of the *New York Evening Post*, William Cullen Bryant, to a party held in their honor at his home. Lathers sold his house to the pres-ident of the First National Bank of Charleston, Andrew Simonds, in 1874 and returned to New York. Simonds used the house for busi-ness purposes and entertaining political friends.

The house at 20 S. Battery Street changed hands several times in the twentieth century. The present owners of the property are Mr. and Mrs. Drayton Hastie, who established the Battery Carriage House Inn on the site in 1976. The eleven-room inn is located in an outbuilding overlooking the garden. The house has been used in the filming of *North and South* and *Queen*.

Mrs. Hastie has a personal connection to the old house. In the 1890s, her grandmother, Sara Calhoun Simonds, lived in the house. When she was a little girl, Sara climbed on a limb and jumped onto the roof. As she was walking along the roof, her feet slipped, and she fell through the ballroom skylight. Fortunately, she landed upside down in a huge crystal chandelier.

The inn's supernatural guest began making an appearance shortly after the Battery Carriage House Inn opened for business. The first ghost to make an appearance was that of one of the young soldiers who defended Charleston against the Yankees. A number of families gathered up their valuables and traveled 120 miles to the capital city of Columbia, which they mistakenly assumed would be a safe refuge. One company of nine Confederate soldiers was ordered to stay and destroy the hundreds of pounds of munitions, and the house was converted into a temporary barracks. According to local lore, one young soldier who was handling one of the highly explosive shells was accidentally blown to pieces.

The staff at the inn assumes that their ghost was one of the nine soldiers who spent the night in the carriage house because he seems to have made one of the rooms his permanent home. Kathy Jo Connor, a concierge at the inn, tells the story of a couple who discovered on August 8, 1992, that they were not the only ones in Room 8: "The man had heard that the room was haunted, but he did not believe in ghosts, so he and his wife went right to sleep. Late that night, he got the feeling that someone was staring at him when he was sleeping, so he woke up and saw the apparition of a headless torso floating over the end of his bed. The man started looking around the room for a projector because he thought the bed and breakfast was putting on a show to scare him. [When he realized that there was no projector in the room], he got curious and scooted to the end of the bed. He put his hand right through the apparition! Just as he did this, he knew he'd done something wrong because his whole arm became cold. He turned his arm sideways and tried to pull it out of the apparition. As he did this, he could feel the wool fabric of the soldier's uniform. When he finally pulled his arm all of the way out, the ghost moaned and disappeared."

On Thanksgiving weekend in 2003, another couple discovered that Room 8 came with an unexpected bonus. Connor checked in the man and woman at 5:00 P.M.: "Everything was fine. They loved the room. I came back upstairs [a little while later], and I saw them throw their bags over the top of the railing." The first thought that went through Connor's mind was, "What's going on there?" Connor said the couple picked up their bags and walked quickly to the lobby. The man said, "We'd like to check out. You did not tell us the place is haunted. We can't stay here. We want our money back!" Taken aback by the fear on the man's face, Connor said, "I'm very sorry. We're on a 'don't ask, don't tell' basis." As Connor was refunding their money, the man explained that they had no sooner laid their bags on the bed when the blinds closed by themselves. The man tried to open the blinds with no success. "It was as if something was holding the blinds back," the man explained.

Another much less threatening spirit haunts Room 10. The ghost story centers on a young man from a well-to-do family who lived in

Charleston at the turn of the century. When the man was eighteen, he fell in love with a young woman who agreed to marry him. His parents were upset when they learned of their son's engagement because they had wanted him to attend Yale University. Unwilling to go against his parents' wishes, the young man reluctantly put off his marriage. "A week after he left for school, his girlfriend ran off with a local boy and got married," Connor said. "His family didn't have the heart to tell him, so when he got back to Charleston and found it out, he was so depressed that he got dressed up in his best suit and he fell from the top of the house into the garden. People said he 'fell' because they didn't say 'suicide' back then."

The story goes that the young man's spirit has taken up permanent residence in Room 10. He has been christened the "Gentleman Ghost," Connor explains, "because he only shows himself to women, he's nicely dressed, and when women let him know that they don't want him there, he leaves." The Gentleman Ghost was seen by twin sisters who checked into Room 10 on their birthday. "One sister lay on the bed, and the other sister propped up a chair against the door and was reading a book," Connor said. "While she was reading, she saw the apparition of a tall, slender man enter the room through the wall and lie down on the bed with her sister." Connor says that the lady was not afraid until the ghost put his arm around her sister. "She walked over and started shaking her so she could see the ghost. Finally, her sister woke up and screamed. When she screamed, the Gentleman Ghost got out of the bed, took a bow, and exited through the wall that he had come through. [Later], they said they could see the outline of his suit, but it was like someone had taken an eraser and erased his face."

One of the more recent appearances of the Gentleman Ghost took place on April 4, 2004. A couple had come to the Battery Carriage House Inn to spend their third anniversary. While the wife was alone upstairs in Room 10, her husband was downstairs talking to Connor: "That night, I was working, and the husband was downstairs asking me a million questions. We didn't know at the time that his wife was experiencing the Gentleman Ghost upstairs. What happened to her was very different from what everybody else had said. She said she was sitting on her bed watching TV, and she kept seeing shadows pass her window." The woman assumed that her husband was standing outside smoking a cigarette. She realized her error when the shadow suddenly came into the room and showed up on the wall. "She then smelled cologne, a soapy, clean cologne," Connor said. "The only thing she could relate that smell to is Old Spice. It wasn't like her husband's [cologne], so she soon put two and two together. She got scared and opened the door, and the apparition disappeared." The woman was halfway down the stairs when she met her husband coming up. Surprisingly, neither the woman nor her husband was frightened by what had happened to her. "They went back to the room, went to sleep that night, checked out the next morning, told us the story, and wrote up a nice little letter."

According to Connor, the cleaning ladies have sensed the presence of entities in two rooms: "They'll get into the bathtubs in Rooms 8 and 10 and start cleaning the shower, and the shower will come on suddenly and soak them. That's happened a couple of times, and the cleaning ladies swear they didn't bump the nozzle."

The ghosts in the Battery Carriage House Inn are unusual in that they appear to congregate in different rooms. "The more they congregate, the more things happen," Connor said. "Room 3 used to be the original wine cellar in the main house, so we can understand why ghosts would congregate there more than anywhere else. It's one of my favorite rooms. It's the only room that has a sitting area and a bedroom. It has a wall mirror, so it looks larger." People who have stayed in that room have had problems with their cell phones turning off and on. "They have also seen a blue light in that room. The light can't come from an outside source because there are no windows," Connor said.

With help from the tour guides who thrill tourists with tales of Charleston's ghosts, the Battery Carriage House Inn has become known as one of the city's most haunted places. In fact, one could say that the spirit that haunts Room 8 is probably one of the most terrifying ghosts in the entire nation. Regardless of whether or not one believes the ghost stories, it cannot be denied that in war-torn cities like Charleston, the Civil War is as much a part of the present as of the past.

Ghost Pirates of Battery Park

Battery Park on the waterfront is one of the most picturesque sites in Charleston. Weary tourists resting in the shade of the stately oaks are surrounded by mementos of Charleston's past, including cannons, cannonballs, estates, antebellum mansions, and a clear view of Fort Sumter. In the eighteenth and nineteenth centuries, Battery Park was known as White Point Gardens, owing to the bleached oyster shells that once blanketed the area. In the early 1700s, White Point Gardens was a low, marshy area that was frequented by pirates. Dozens of pirates were hanged at this spot and left dangling from the oaks as an object lesson to would-be buccaneers. Some residents of Charleston believe that the ghosts of pirates who lie buried beneath the waterline are still walking among the oak trees of Battery Park.

In the early 1700s, piracy was a serious problem in and around Charleston. Pirates lurked in the channel, waiting for unsuspecting merchant vessels to pass by as they entered or left the harbor. The colonial governor of South Carolina, Robert Johnson, reached an end to his patience in May of 1718 when Blackbeard captured nine merchant ships and kidnapped several prominent citizens. Johnson authorized a military hero named Colonel William Rhett to lead an expedition against the pirates. In August and September, Colonel Rhett pursued pirates along South Carolina's coast. Then on September 27, Colonel Rhett's forces encountered the *Royal James*, a pirate ship commanded by a friend of Blackbeard's, Stede Bonnet. At the time, Bonnet was anchoring at Cape Fear to clean the hull of his ship. Following a fierce five-hour battle, Colonel Rhett defeated the vastly outnumbered pirates and brought Bonnet and his crew back to Charleston on October 3, 1718, to stand trial.

Stede Bonnet, known far and wide as "the gentleman pirate," embarked on a life of crime in the summer of 1717, he claimed, to escape the nagging of his wife. He had been aboard Blackbeard's flagship in May 1718 when he plundered the nine ships outside Charleston harbor. After their capture, Bonnet's crew awaited trial in the Guard House at the Half Moon Battery. Because of his reputation as a gentleman Bonnet was given a room at the house of Marshall Partridge. Bonnet took advantage of his "low-security" confinement and escaped by dressing in women's clothing. A few days later, he was again apprehended by Colonel Rhett. Bonnet bided his time by writing a letter to the governor, pledging to reform if pardoned, but his plea for clemency was denied. He and thirty-four other pirates were tried between October 28 and November 12. Judge Nicholas Trot sentenced Bonnet and twenty-nine of his cohorts to death by hanging.

The public hanging took place at White Point Gardens on December 10, 1718. Some people say that Bonnet's body "danced" at the end of the rope because he did not drop far enough to break his neck. The bodies were left hanging for four days. They were then dumped in the marshes along Vanderhorst Creek. The authorities hoped that the stench from the rotting corpses would be vile enough to deter any other pirate crews who happened to be rowing up the creek on their way to town.

Many people claim to have encountered the restless spirits of the pirates executed at White Point Gardens. It is said that the ghosts of the long-dead pirates walk around the oak trees and scream at passersby. Local legend has it that if one stands at the foot of Water Street where Vanderhorst Creek once flowed down to the harbor and stares out into the water when the moon is high, he or she can see the pale, bloated faces of pirates floating just below the surface of the water, staring up at the moon. The frequent appearance of the pirates' ghosts over the centuries could be their way of protesting the sacrilegious manner in which their bodies were disposed.

Eastern South Carolina

THE COASTLINE OF SOUTH CAROLINA IS 187 MILES LONG. THE MOST distinguishing feature of the Grand Strand, which forms the northern part of the coastline, is its nearly sixty miles of unbroken beach stretching from Georgetown to Myrtle Beach. The area south of Winyah Bay is covered primarily by saltwater marshes. A number of natural ports can also be found along the coastline. The large number of oval-shaped bays has led some geologists to conclude that this area was bombarded by a meteor shower millions of years ago. The coastline is also dotted with a number of islands, including Pawley's Island, Edisto Island, and Kiawah Island.

Alice Flagg's Eternal Search

Situated in a grove of white oaks just south of Myrtle Beach on Highway 17 is a beautiful antebellum home called the Hermitage. Built by Dr. Allard Belin Flagg in 1848, the comparatively modest mansion features a front porch with columns four feet in diameter. The front steps of the porch were built of bricks that had once been used as ballast in ships. The front door features glass sidelights and a glass transom. The floors consist of twenty-foot lengths of heart pine. One of the two bedrooms on the second floor was occupied in the mid-nineteenth century by Dr. Flagg's vivacious younger sister,

Alice. According to legend, Alice's melancholy spirit still walks the halls of the Hermitage.

Alice Flagg was, in many ways, a typical planter's daughter in the Low Country. She was waited on by servants, dined on gourmet dishes, and dressed in the latest fashions. However, after she turned sixteen, it became clear to her family that she was more headstrong than many young women of the time. According to one version of the story, she made the acquaintance of a young turpentine merchant while on a shopping trip. Within a few months, she fell hopelessly in love with the young man. One day, he came to call on Alice at the Hermitage. Dr. Flagg escorted the young man to the garden and spoke with him. Before long, Dr. Flagg became convinced that the young man was far too unrefined for someone of Alice's social standing. When the interview was over, Dr. Flagg dismissed Alice's suitor without allowing him to see her. In a variant of the story, Alice's boyfriend rode up to the Hermitage just as she was stepping into her carriage. Dr. Flagg rushed out of the house, climbed into the carriage next to Alice, and took the reins. He then told the young man that he was welcome to ride on his horse alongside the carriage if he wished.

Dr. Flagg decided that the best way to end his sister's romance was to send her to boarding school in Charleston. He did not realize that Alice had already become engaged to the young man whom he believed was so much beneath her. She was able to conceal her engagement from her mother and brother by wearing her engagement ring on a ribbon around her neck beneath her blouse. Probably the happiest time in the girl's life was the Spring Ball, where the debutantes were presented to society. Because her mother and brother were unable to attend, Alice, radiant in a beautiful white gown, was able to dance the entire evening with her fiancé.

The next day, Alice became ill and took to her bed. School officials soon realized that the red glow in Alice's cheeks the night before was actually a symptom of the fever that was raging through the countryside. Word was sent to Dr. Flagg to take Alice home as soon as he could. Slowed down by swollen rivers, Dr. Flagg and a servant arrived at the school four days later in a carriage laden with medicine. When Dr. Flagg's carriage returned to the Hermitage, Alice was carried up the stairs to her bedroom. While Dr. Flagg was examining her, he discovered the ring hanging from a ribbon under her blouse. In a fit of rage, Dr. Flagg ripped the ring from Alice's neck and tossed it in a nearby creek. For the next week, Alice begged her visitors to find her ring and return it to her. When she could muster the strength, Alice staggered around her bedroom, looking for the lost ring. Her guilt-ridden brother presented her a different ring in the hope she would think it was her engagement ring, but she could tell that it was a poor substitute. After Alice finally succumbed to her illness, she was buried in a temporary grave in the yard until her mother arrived from the mountains, where she had gone to escape the fever. Alice Flagg now rests in the cemetery of the All Saints Waccamaw Church. Her grave is marked by a marble slab on which is engraved the name "Alice."

For more than one hundred and fifty years, Alice's spirit has been an active presence at the Hermitage. Friends and relatives of the current owners have reportedly seen the ghostly image of a pretty young girl in a white dress in the mirror in her bedroom. Her spirit has also been seen entering and leaving the Hermitage through the front door. When Alice appears, she is usually wearing a white gown and clutching one hand to her chest. However, Alice might have also taken the form of a wispy, misty entity that floated out of her bedroom and up the stairs late one night. Alice's ghost has also been sighted walking around her temporary gravesite and around the cemetery of the All Saints Waccamaw Church. For years, teenagers have tried to summon Alice's spirit by walking around her gravesite thirteen times. It is also said that if a girl runs around Alice's grave nine times, her ring will vanish from her ring finger. Locals say that Alice's ghost will continue to wander around the cemetery and the Hermitage until she finally locates the ring her lover gave her so many years ago.

The Gray Man of Pawleys Island

Pawleys Island in the tidelands of Georgetown County lies on the southern end of the Grand Strand. Pawleys Island was first settled by the Waccamaw and Winyah Indians. One of the first European settlers was George Pawley, whose rice plantations made him a wealthy man. In the early 1800s, a number of plantation families moved to the island from Georgetown in an effort to escape the extreme heat and malaria-carrying mosquitoes on the mainland.

The sturdy summer houses they built in what came to be known as the "Pawleys style" had wraparound porches and gabled roofs. Some of them, such as Beachaven, are still standing today.

Many of the Georgetown families lost their plantations in the devastation wrought by hurricanes and the Civil War, but they kept their homes on Pawleys Island. In 1989, Hurricane Hugo swept away some of these cottages, which were replaced by more upscale homes. Today, Pawleys Island, population 138, is home to a cluster of cypress-sided cottages and inns that has moved some visitors to describe the little town as "arrogantly shabby." The island is also home to a friendly ghost known as "the Gray Man."

The legend of the Gray Man is the most commonly related legend in Georgetown County. Several variants of the tale are still told to this day. The oldest version of the story takes place in the eighteenth century. A young woman from a wealthy Charleston family fell in love with her handsome cousin, who was reputed to be a rake. Her parents tried to end the romance by sending the young man to France. When the girl received word a few months later that her cousin had been killed in a duel, she sank into a deep depression. A year later, she met and fell in love with a wealthy young planter from the Waccamaw area. This time, her father approved of the match, and the couple was married. They loved spending the winter months on a large estate on Pawleys Island.

The couple's idyllic existence ended during the Revolutionary War when the young woman's husband rode off to join the forces of Francis Marion, the "Swamp Fox." In the summer of 1778, while the young woman was staying in the couple's summer home on Pawley's Island, she received word about a shipwreck on the island. Her servants were dispatched to the site of the wreck, where they found only one survivor. They dragged the half-drowned man out of the surf and brought him to the main house. As the slaves carried him into the house, the young woman recognized the bedraggled man as her lost love, the cousin who had reportedly died in Europe. Some people say that he staggered off into the woods in a delirious state and was never heard from again. Others say that he died of yellow fever on his way to Charleston. Over the years, the cousin's apparition reportedly continued to watch over the woman and her husband when they vacationed at Pawleys Island.

In another commonly told variant of the legend, a young girl whose father owned a house on Pawleys Island was engaged to a young man who had gone off to fight with General Washington in the Revolutionary War. Meanwhile, she kept a vigil at the window, waiting for her fiancé to return. After several months, the young man returned to Georgetown by ship. After disembarking, he was so eager to see the girl on Pawleys Island that he took a hazardous route across the marsh instead of using one of the causeways. He had not ridden very far before his horse became mired in the mud. His servant watched helplessly as the young man sank out of sight. Following the man's funeral, the girl was taking a walk along the beach, just as she and her lover had done on moonlit nights, when a strange, grayish-colored figure that resembled her fiancé suddenly appeared before her. In a quavering voice, he told her to leave the island with her family before an oncoming hurricane destroyed the island. Terrified by what she had seen and heard, the girl ran home and told her father that a hurricane was on its way. Even though the story she told him was unbelievable, he decided that the prudent thing to do in light of this information was to move his family inland. Later that same day, a hurricane pummeled Pawleys Island, destroying many of the homes there. The young woman's house was one of the few that were spared.

For generations, the Gray Man has appeared on Pawleys Island just before hurricanes to warn the residents of impending danger. The man was seen in 1822, 1893, 1916, 1954, 1955, and 1995, just before a hurricane hit the island. The legend is so famous, in fact, that when he makes his next appearance on Pawleys Island, everyone will know that vacation time is over.

The Lucas Bay Light

The legend behind Lucas Bay's most famous ghost story reflects the intense fear that Union troops under the command of William Tecumseh Sherman instilled in the civilian population of South Carolina during the Civil War. Many Yankee soldiers carried with them an intense hatred of South Carolina because, as the first state to leave the Union, it had started the conflict. As Sherman's soldiers marched through South Carolina in February 1865, they burned and pillaged with a ferocity that they had not shown in Georgia. After the burning of the state capital, Columbia, on February 17, Confederate general Pierre Gustave Toutant Beauregard ordered the evacuation of Charleston. Panic soon spread to the citizens of other coastal cities and towns, most of whom were female. One small town, Lucas Bay, was located next to Bucksport, which was certain to be target of the Union army because of its shipping and milling facilities. Fearful that the Yankee soldiers who attacked Bucksport would turn their attention to Lucas Bay, the women did their best to hide their valuables. One young woman's unsuccessful attempt to protect her most precious possession is preserved in the story of the Lucas Bay Light.

A woman whose name has been lost to history bundled up her baby and walked over to a nearby bridge that spanned a ricefield canal. She placed the sleeping child under the bridge and returned home to protect her house and its furnishings from Sherman's troops. That night, a severe thunderstorm hit the area. Worried that her baby would drown in the rising waters of the canal, the woman hastily wrapped her head in a shawl and rushed over to the bridge. As the rain fell in torrents, the woman carefully made her way down the slippery clay bank. She was almost under the bridge when she slipped and hit her head on one of the bridge supports. Dazed and bleeding, she tried to stand up, but she lost her balance, fell into the raging water, and drowned. Her baby drowned as well in the rising floodwaters.

For more than one hundred and fifty years, a strange ball of light has been seen on the bridge along Lucas Bay Road. Residents say that the ball starts out as a small red orb on the bridge and then, as it travels across the bridge, expands to the size of a basketball. It continues traveling down the road until it blinks out. It is said that the light is the lantern the woman held as she tried in vain to rescue her baby.

The Lucas Bay Light usually makes an appearance on rainy nights, just before dusk. In July 2005, a carload of teenagers spotted the light on Little Lamb Road. As they were driving along, one of the boys noticed a light similar to the burning end of a cigarette following them. When he looked again, the light had expanded to the size of a beach ball. The teenagers became so alarmed that the driver gunned the engine. As the car careened down the road into a fog bank, one of the girls in the car screamed. At that moment, the glowing ball of light vanished.

Many of the ghostly bridges in Southern folklore involve mothers and babies. Some of these structures, known to locals as "crybaby bridges," get their name from an unmarried, pregnant woman who jumps off the bridge and commits suicide. Teenagers hoping to catch a glimpse of the poor woman's spirit place candy bars on the bridge rail and honk their horn several times. Unlike the pregnant women who kill themselves and their unborn children, the woman who is the focus of the Lucas Bay ghost light story is memorialized today because of her heroic efforts to rescue her child.

The Mournful Mistress of Medway Plantation

Medway Plantation was established in 1687 on a 21,000-acre tract in present-day Berkeley County by Jan Van Arssens. The one-story stucco house he built with stair-step gables was reminiscent of the homes found in the French region of Brittany, down the English Channel from Van Arrsens' native Netherlands. Following Van Arrsens' death, his widow married Thomas Smith, who became sole heir of the property when she died in 1689. After Thomas Smith died at age forty-six, new owners made a number of alterations to the estate. Jane Dubose, wife of Theodore Samuel Dubose, planted the large oaks and ornamental trees in a pattern around the house. A second story was added to the house as well. Peter Gaillard Stoney, who purchased Medway in 1833, added an asymmetrical wing in 1855. Stoney also set up a brickmaking operation and a racetrack on the estate. Because he was an avid deer hunter, Stoney fenced in large tracts of land to be used as hunting parks. Medway Plantation remained in the Stoney family until 1930, when it was sold to Mr. and Mrs. Sidney Legendre of New Orleans. Today, Medway is the oldest house in South Carolina. Legend has it that Medway is also home to at least two spirits.

Both male and female ghosts are said to walk the halls of Medway. One of these spirits is the ghost of an elderly man. He is usually seen smoking an invisible pipe in the upstairs south bedroom. The ghost has been identified as the spirit of Jan Van Arrsens, who feels comfortable in the old house because the changes made by subsequent owners were in keeping with the Dutch architectural tradition.

The other spirit is the ghost of a young woman. In her book *Charleston Ghosts*, Margaret Rhett Martin says that the apparition is the ghost of a young bride who was visiting Medway with her husband. When he announced that he was going off with a group of hunters, she was filled with a sense of foreboding. She begged the young man to stay in the house with her, but he laughed at her tears and rode off with the rest of the hunting party. For the remainder of the day, the young woman returned to the north window, where she gazed out over the rolling hills of the plantation in search of her husband. After darkness fell and the hunting party returned, the bride's worst fears were realized when she stared at the glum faces of her husband's hunting companions as they carried her husband's corpse into the house. She rushed over to the stretcher where her husband lay and cried uncontrollably. The heartbroken young woman was taken home, where she died a few days later. It is said that she maintains her lonely vigil at the north window, where her pale face can still be seen staring out of the small windowpanes. Later occupants of the house claimed that they could also hear the rustling of her gown as she walked past the window.

Today, Medway is a lonely remnant of Goose Creek plantation society. Vestiges of the racetrack and the gardens planted by the wives of previous owners still remain. One section of the plantation—Smithfield—retains the name of the second owner of the estate. The most intriguing aspects of the old plantation, however, are the ghost legends, which are certain to remain as long as Medway is still standing.

Hampton Plantation's Suicidal Spirit

Daniel Horry built the original part of Hampton Plantation on six hundred acres he had purchased from Anthony Bonneau in 1744. Daniel Huger Horry inherited the rice plantation from his father in 1762 and expanded the house. In 1778, relatives and friends of Daniel and his wife, Harriott Pickney Horry, sought refuge at the plantation during the Revolutionary War. Two years later, after the British captured Charleston, British soldiers searched Hampton

Plantation twice. During the second visit, the British forced Horry to take a loyalty oath to the British. After the Americans won the war and discovered the loyalty oath, Horry's property was confiscated, but his in-laws, the Pinckneys, arranged for him to pay an amercement tax so that he could keep his plantation.

After Daniel Huger Horry died in November 1785, his son, Daniel, inherited the estate. However, Daniel Horry changed his name and permanently moved to Europe, and his mother and grandmother took over the estate in his absence. In 1797, Harriott's daughter, also named Harriott, moved into the plantation house with her husband, Frederick Rutledge. She inherited the property in 1830 after her mother died. Henry Middleton Rutledge, the younger Harriott's grandson, managed the plantation after the Civil War. In 1876, Henry Middleton Rutledge married Margaret Hamilton Seabrook. Their son Archibald worked as a professor of English at Mercersburg Academy in Pennsylvania from 1904 until 1937. Archibald, who was appointed the Poet Laureate of South Carolina, returned to Hampton Plantation in 1937, and in his will he bequeathed the plantation to the South Carolina State Park Service. He may have unwittingly deeded the family ghost to the state as well.

The ghost of Hampton Plantation is allegedly the spirit of John Henry Rutledge, one of the sons of Harriott and Frederick Rutledge. In 1830, twenty-one-year-old John Henry fell in love with a girl from Georgetown. Her father was a pharmacist, a profession which the Rutledges looked upon with disdain. Eventually, the girl married another man. Despondent, John Henry went into the library one March day and shot himself in the head with a sawed-off shotgun. The gunshot was not immediately fatal. Several days later, he finally passed away. Because John Henry Rutledge was a suicide, he could not be buried in the cemetery, so his family buried him outside the front door.

Most of the paranormal activity in Hampton Manor focuses on the bedroom where John Henry Rutledge passed away. Several years after John Henry's tragic death, a servant heard a chair rocking upstairs. She did not recall anyone being on the second story at the time, so she ran upstairs to investigate. To her horror, the rocking chair John Henry was sitting in when he shot himself was rocking by itself. Over the years, visitors have heard the chair rocking in the library, accompanied by the sound of a man sobbing.

Other strange things have occurred at Hampton Plantation as well. A number of visitors reported hearing what is believed to be the sound of a baby being dragged from a northwest to a southeast corner of the upstairs bedroom. One of the managers of Hampton Plantation said that several nights after he turned off the lights in the house, the lights came back on as he was driving away. Doors that he thought he had locked at closing time somehow unlocked themselves.

Some experts in the paranormal believe that John Henry Rutledge's ghost haunts the library and bedroom of Hampton Hall because suicides are denied entrance into heaven. Indeed, the ghost does seem to be a melancholy presence in the house, a spirit that has condemned itself to an eternity of mystery. The fact that he does not appear to be a threat to anyone but himself has not prevented some people from being afraid in the house. Tour guide Sarah Tyler said, "The other interpreter refuses to stay here after dark. I don't doubt that something is happening, but I've never seen it."

The Headless Sentry of Wedgefield Plantation Manor

Wedgefield Plantation, which is located just north of Georgetown, was established on one of the first land grants in South Carolina. The first plantation house was a one-and-a-half-story cottage. The 610-acre plantation was in full operation by the early 1750s. In 1762, a prominent planter-merchant named Samuel Wragg purchased the plantation and replaced the original plantation house with a new manor that was very simple in design. The original cottage became the home of the overseer. Wragg, who also owned homes in Georgetown and Charleston, was a wealthy man who entertained his business associates in his beautiful home. He was also heavily involved in local politics. Because Wragg had profited immensely from his business connections with England, he became a Tory after the British occupied Georgetown. His headstrong daughter, however, was not only loyal to the colonies; she became a spy for General Francis Marion. The wide gulf between the political ideologies of father and daughter set the stage for a violent incident at Wedge-

field Manor that has been memorialized in folklore for more than two centuries.

In 1781, every house in Georgetown was used by the British to quarter their troops, even the houses of Loyalists. Wedgefield Manor was selected as the perfect place to house American prisoners. Before long, word reached Francis Marion that the father of one of his soldiers was being held at Wedgefield Manor along with four women and two old men. Because the soldier's father had been present when Marion was formulating his plans for attacking the British, the old man's release became a top priority. Marion dispatched one of his men to make contact with Wragg's daughter in order to find out exactly where the old man was being held on the plantation. The girl told him that the old man, his daughter, and his niece had been held prisoner in the servants' quarters but were moved to an unknown location. She assured the soldier, though, that their new quarters must be close by. The next day, she informed him that the old man and his family were being temporarily housed in her father's servants' house. A few days later, the girl left a message next to a headstone in a nearby cemetery stating that she, her father, and most of the soldiers stationed at the plantation were planning to attend a party at the Mansfield plantation, located just down the road from Wedgefield. The prisoners would be guarded by a single sentry.

The following Thursday at twilight, Marion and a party of his men galloped up the drive of Wedgefield Manor. Thinking that the riders were his own men, the sentry ran down the steps to greet them. When the sentry realized that the horsemen were Francis Marion's soldiers, he drew his pistol and fired at one of the men. A moment later, one of Marion's cavalrymen rode up behind the sentry and lopped off his head with his saber. The sentry's corpse stumbled for a few seconds and then collapsed in a quivering heap upon the ground. Marion's party freed the American prisoners, much to the joy of the son of the old man. The triumph of the occasion was overshadowed by the memory of the horrible death throes of the unfortunate sentry.

After the release of the prisoners from Wedgefield, the decapitated corpse of the British soldier was buried in the garden. Seven weeks later, Wragg's daughter was awakened by the sound of horses' hooves thundering down the drive. Staring out of her bedroom window, she saw a headless British soldier walk up the front steps of the manor and vanish. In the next few months, other family members witnessed the headless corpse of the sentry staggering around the garden with a pistol in its hand. The soldier was also seen standing in the front yard. Usually, the appearance of the British sentry was preceded by the clanking of chains across the porch or the pounding of the hoofbeats of phantom horses just before nightfall. The sentry was sometimes seen on moonlit nights with his head sitting on his shoulders, pacing back and forth across the porch.

In the 1930s, the Wedgefield plantation house was torn down. A new mansion was built in its place. The headless apparition does not appear as often as it used to. The ghostly guard lives on, though, in the old legends that are told in Georgetown. Whenever a strange noise is heard in the house, there is always someone who wonders if it is the headless sentry's way of making his presence known in his new surroundings.

The Seneca Guns

Mysterious booming sounds have disrupted the tranquility of the Low Country since the eighteenth century. The thunderous rumble, which sailors stationed in Charleston harbor during World War II likened to the sound of cannon fire, is usually heard several times every summer in the daylight hours. When the booms roll in off the ocean, houses shake to their foundations. Pictures fall off the walls, windows rattle, and glasses crash to the floor.

This strange phenomenon was given the nickname "the Seneca Guns" in the mid-nineteenth century, following the publication of a short story by James Fenimore Cooper. "The Lake Gun" was written by Cooper in 1850 at the request of George E. Wood, who included it in a volume of miscellaneous stories and poems called *The Parthenon*. In the story, Cooper describes the booming sounds heard on New York's Seneca Lake as being "deep, hollow, distant, and imposing." According to Cooper's story, the legend of the Seneca Guns is closely connected with the fate of a brash young Seneca Indian brave named See-wise, who boasted before the tribal council that the red men made the world themselves, and for themselves, and that they could do with it as they pleased. The Great

Spirit punished See-wise for his blasphemy by condemning him to float among the salmon, the trout, and the eels in Seneca Lake for a thousand years. The Lake Gun is the booming voice of the Great Spirit, forbidding See-wise to fish.

The Seneca Guns were heard in Charleston during the week of August 2, 2003. At 1:30 P.M., Low Country communities were rocked by what sounded like a very loud sonic boom. For the rest of the afternoon, the Charleston Police Department received phone calls from James Island, Wadmalaw, and Daniel Island. None of the callers saw any fires or explosions. Earthquake experts at Charleston Southern University and at the University of South Carolina reported that their seismographs recorded no earthquakes at the time. Spokespersons for the military said that no planes that could make a sonic boom were flying in or around the area affected by the boom.

A number of theories have been offered to explain the source of the Seneca Guns. Sonic booms from military aircraft may have been responsible for some of the booming sounds in recent years. Naval gunfire can travel extraordinary distances under certain atmospheric conditions. In fact, the Navy admitted that it was responsible for similar booms heard off the coast of Virginia in the 1970s. Some experts believe that the booms are produced by small, shallow earthquakes. Less plausible explanations include methane released from the ocean floor, sinkholes forming in limestone, alien spaceships, shifts of tectonic plates, meteors exploding in the atmosphere, and remnants of atomic bomb testing. Because the booms have acquired the name "Seneca Guns," the story has been passed down for more than a century that the ghosts of Indians are firing their guns to disturb the descendants of the early pioneers. Who can say that the folklore account is less plausible than some of the scientific explanations?

The Dead Ringer
of Litchfield Plantation

Litchfield Plantation is one of the oldest rice plantations on the Waccamaw River. Peter Simon built the plantation house in 1740 on lands he had been granted by King George II. After Peter died on November 10, 1794, his plantation was divided between his two sons, Peter and John. In 1796, Litchfield was purchased by Daniel Tucker from Georgetown. Under the ownership of Daniel's eldest son, John, Litchfield Plantation thrived, producing one million pounds of rice per year by 1850. Litchfield Plantation remained in the Tucker family until 1897, when it was purchased by Breslauer, Lachicotte and Company. The plantation changed hands several times in the twentieth century before it became an upscale gated community in 1969. Over the next eleven years, thirty villas, seven condominiums, and thirteen single-family homes were constructed. It has since undergone further development. Litchfield Plantation has changed considerably over the years, but, according to legend, the nightly routine of one of the plantation's early owners has not.

Dr. Henry Massingberd Tucker was the most colorful of all the owners of Litchfield Plantation. Dr. Tucker, who served in the Confederate army for four years, was an expert marksman who won a number of tournaments at the Georgetown Rifle Club. He was also a very religious man who dismantled the old All Saints Church and moved it to his property. Unable to control his temper at times, he is said to have cut the rations of food and tobacco from slaves who refused to attend church. He was an impatient man as well. When returning by horseback from midnight house calls, Dr. Tucker became very angry if the gatekeeper was not at his post. Sometimes, he beat on the gate bell furiously with his riding crop. If the gatekeeper still did not show, the disgruntled doctor tied his horse to the bellpost, climbed over the split log fence, and walked home.

For years after his death, subsequent owners of the plantation claimed to have heard the clanging of the bell late at night. One of the owners of the plantation became so tired of being awakened in the middle of the night that he had the bell removed from the gate. A few people witnessed the doctor's apparition walking up the darkened back stairway. His ghost has also been seen in a second-floor guest room that was Dr. Tucker's bedroom. In her book *Best Ghost Tales of South Carolina*, Terrance Zepke says that one of the former owners of the plantation, Arthur Lachicotte, often heard footsteps in the house when he was the only one present.

Today, the plantation house is part of a luxurious resort, offering comfortable accommodations in its villas and cottages. The resort also offers guests fine dining at the Carriage House Club and the relaxing atmosphere of the three-story oceanfront beach clubhouse on nearby Pawleys Island. Visitors while away the hours in the heated pool and the clubhouse cabana. However, from a paranormal perspective, the spacious suites of the Plantation House are the resort's greatest attraction, mainly because of the prospect of being treated to an appearance of Dr. Tucker's ghost.

Strawberry Chapel Graveyard

Strawberry Chapel takes its name from a bluff on the east side of the Cooper River's west branch. It is the only visible remnant of the town of Childsburg, which was laid out on land donated by Englishman James Child in 1701. Strawberry Chapel was constructed in 1725 by an Act of Assembly to St. John's Biggin Church. "Chapels of ease" were used as substitute churches for congregants unable to travel to a parish's main church. Strawberry Chapel was unique among such chapels, however, in that it operated as a full parish church. The town around the church was abandoned in 1815, and the land was absorbed by a local plantation. Today, in the graveyard connected to Strawberry Chapel, one can find a number of historically significant names. Locals believe that a few ghosts can be found there as well.

The Strawberry Chapel graveyard is said to be haunted by a variety of spirits. Many people have been overcome with depression as soon as they enter the graveyard. Some say that the spirits of six children can be seen playing among the tombstones. Late in the evening, visitors have heard the sound of childish laughter and giggling. The sobbing of a child, most likely the ghost of Little Mistress Chicken, has been heard as well. A tombstone in the section next to Strawberry Chapel is said to be exceedingly warm to the touch, even in winter. Teenagers looking for late-night thrills have reported seeing the image of a gray-clad figure standing on a nearby dock on the Cooper River.

I visited Strawberry Chapel on July 28, 2004. At the time, the sun was beginning to set. With a sense of urgency, my wife and I walked briskly through the old graveyard, trying to get as many photographs as we could before darkness fell. When I stopped to peer into the gaping mouth of an empty tomb, I suddenly realized how still the sultry air was. The phrase "quiet as a tomb" assumed new significance for me at that moment. As I walked along, reading the epitaphs on centuries-old tombstones, I had the uneasy feeling that I was being watched. We had not been in the graveyard for more than fifteen minutes before my wife informed me that she was ready to leave because the graveyard had become "too creepy." Walking through the deepening shadows to my car, I had the distinct sensation that something was right behind me. I turned around twice just to make sure that no one was there. It was with a profound sense of relief that we drove away from Strawberry Chapel graveyard.

The overwhelming feeling of depression that swept over me as I left Strawberry Chapel Graveyard was due at least in part to the broken and overturned tombstones that were everywhere. Unless visitors pay the buried dead the reverence due them, the vandalism will continue, and Strawberry Chapel Graveyard will become nothing more than a distant memory.

The Ghost of Little Mistress Chicken

Rice Hope Plantation in Moncks Corner hearkens back to the days when rice was one of South Carolina's most important cash crops. Luckins Plantation, as Rice Hope was called in the eighteenth century, was built in 1735 by Charles Read, who had received a grant to construct a ferry not far from Strawberry Chapel. His son, Dr. William Read, turned the plantation into a profitable enterprise. By impounding streams inland a little farther upstream from the plantation, Read was able to control the tides to flood the fields. Charles Read's daughter, who had married a man named Captain Chicken, had a child named Catherine. After Captain Chicken died, Catherine and her mother moved back to Luckins Plantation. Not long after the death of her first husband, Catherine's mother married a prosperous plantation owner named Mr. Ball, and Catherine was sent to a boarding school in Childsbury. The school was run by a cruel schoolmaster named Monsieur Dutarque. The fate of young Catherine Chicken has been memorialized in a local legend that still horrifies listeners more than three centuries later.

After the original plantation burned, Rice Hope was rebuilt in 1840 on its foundation. U.S. Senator John S. Frelinghuysen of New Jersey reopened the house in 1929. It was turned into an inn in 1987. The old bed-and-breakfast, with its five guest rooms and two-hundred-year-old formal garden, overlooks the Cooper River. Lou Edens, the proprietor of the bed-and-breakfast, has been regaling guests with the sad tale of the girl known locally as "Little Mistress Chicken" for many years. The story begins on an early spring day in 1752. Because of her persistent idleness, eight-year-old Catherine was being forced to stay inside the school and sew a long seam as punishment. "She had a little pet turtle that she had named after her deceased father's boat," Edens said. "She went outside to play with her turtle, and she took the fabric that she was supposed to be sewing with her." After discovering that the child was missing, Mrs. Dutarque feared that some harm might come to the child out in the swampy countryside. With a great deal of prodding, she finally talked her husband into looking for the little girl after he had finished eating dinner. Muttering angrily to himself, Monsieur Dutarque picked up a rope and his horse pistols and marched out the door. He located Catherine not far from the school and decided to teach her a lesson she would never forget. "To punish her, he took her to Strawberry Chapel Churchyard and tied her to a tombstone because he was not a kind man," Edens said. "He forgot her, and darkness came." As the girl struggled to free herself, she began crying uncontrollably.

Late in the night, her cries were heard by a slave who had been visiting a neighboring plantation without permission. "He carried with him what he called a 'Jack-o-me lantern,' which was a gourd with tallow in it," Edens said. "If he got captured in his AWOL behavior, he would light the tallow in his lantern and swing it as if it was a ghost." He traced the source of the whimpering sounds to Strawberry Chapel Churchyard, where he discovered the little girl tied to the tombstone. He did not free her immediately because if he freed her, he would be whipped for leaving his plantation without permission. He would also be committing the egregious crime of touching a white person. While the slave was deliberating, he spotted the lanterns of a search party. The slave stopped the horse of one member of the rescue party and said that he had found Miss Catherine's lifeless body in the churchyard. The rescuers found the tombstone where Catherine was tied, released the girl, and carried her to the waiting arms of her grandmother and her black nanny at Luckins Plantation. While Catherine's mother was being fetched from downriver, her grandmother soothed the little girl by rocking her. By the time her mother arrived, Catherine was lying in bed in a comalike state. While the grief-stricken woman hugged her child and spoke her name, Catherine woke up and, in a strained voice, said, "Don't let them hurt poor M'sieu Dutarque."

Meanwhile, the citizens of Childsbury exacted their own brand of punishment on the Dutarques. "Mrs. Dutarque was put on a ferry and sent across the river, never to come back again," Edens said. "The men were getting ready to whip Monsieur Dutarque when Mr. Ball rode up waving a letter saying that Catherine did not want Monsieur Dutarque harmed. Mr. Dutarque was tied on a mule backwards, and they drummed him out of town. Catherine survived, but she was traumatized by the experience. She married Benjamin Simons of Middleburg Plantation later in life. There's a portrait of her that the Daughters of the American Revolution have. Her face is visibly disfigured, possibly as a result of the ropes that tied her to the tombstone."

For three hundred years, the ghost of the unfortunate girl has haunted Rice Hope Plantation. Catherine's sad little spirit seems to favor the Herron Room, where her grandmother rocked her after her harrowing experience in the Strawberry Chapel Churchyard. According to Edens, the rocking chair still rocks late at night. The chair was moved out of the Herron Room for a while to prevent it from scaring her guests. Despite Eden's efforts to "protect" her visitors from the ghost, guests have sensed the girl's presence in some of the adjoining rooms as well. "There are also reports of hearing doors opening," Edens said. "People have also heard whispering and objects moving. The former owner's daughter saw a girl in a white dress coming up the back stairs, which lead into the ghost room." Eager to determine for herself whether or not the ghost room was really haunted, Edens spent the night there. She did not have a peaceful night. "We couldn't keep the door closed that comes from the back stairway. While I was there, there was a pencil in the drawer on the side table, and it just mysteriously whirled itself around. I decided that I had had my ghost experience and left."

Edens' second ghostly experience occurred one night while she was having a party: "A girl appeared in the parlor. We thought she was a guest who was arriving late, so I told her to come in, thinking she was a guest. I said, 'The party's out on the patio. Why don't you join us?' It was dark by that time. We were having shrub, which is a drink made out of rum, brandy, and orange juice. This girl had on a black, flowing over-blouse and a skirt—I couldn't see her feet. The skirt went to the floor, and the over-blouse went halfway down to her knee. Her hair was pulled back. It cascaded down her back— she could have sat on it. It was cut off real straight at the bottom. Her hair was really noticeable. On my second invitation to join us, she repeated her same sentence, 'No, I just stopped by on my way from Mepkin.' The curious thing was that Mepkin [Abbey] locks its gates around four. As soon as she left, we looked out the window, and we didn't see a vehicle. We have a thing on the gate that rings when a car passes through, and the ding-dong didn't go off."

Edens' first thought was that the girl was the spirit of "Little Mistress Chicken." However, some locals believe that the "party-crashing" ghost was the spirit of the daughter of Clare Boothe Luce and stepdaughter of Henry Luce, the founder of *Time* magazine. In 1936, the Luces acquired nearby Mepkin Plantation and quite possibly attended parties at Rice Hope Plantation. On January 11, 1944, their daughter, Ann Clare Brokaw, a nineteen-year-old senior at Stanford University, was killed in an automobile accident. Clare was so devastated by the loss of her only child that she suffered a nervous breakdown. Convinced that only God could give her a reason to keep on living, she converted to Catholicism in 1946. According to local legend, a dispute with the Episcopalian Church drove Clare to donate a major portion of her 35,000-acre plantation to the Trappist monks of the Abbey of Gethsemani in Kentucky, who then established the present-day Abbey of our Lady of Mepkin in Moncks Corner. "Her daughter was buried at Strawberry Chapel Cemetery," Edens said, "but the church made Clare dig up the girl because she didn't have permission to bury Ann there. After her daughter was 'disinvited' from the cemetery, Clare established a cemetery for Ann at the Mepkin monastery, and she and Henry Luce are buried there too." Edens suspects that the ghost who attended the party was Ann Clare Brokaw because the spirit's fabric seems to have been made from voile, a fabric that was in fashion in the 1940s.

In spite of her two encounters, Edens has no intention of ever leaving Rice Hope Plantation. "I'm never scared here. The ghost is not malicious." One suspects that if "Little Mistress Chicken" ever becomes tired of haunting the old house, Rice Hope Plantation will lose a substantial portion of its charm.

Downstate
South Carolina

THE SOUTHERN TIP OF SOUTH CAROLINA, WHICH LIES WITHIN THE Atlantic Coastal Plain, is one of the most popular tourist destinations in the entire state. Once the haven of wealthy planters, this area is now dotted with a number of luxurious resorts. A good example is Hilton Head Island, which has twelve miles of pristine beaches. Hilton Head attracts thousands of tourists each year with the promise of fine dining, deep-sea fishing, sailing, and numerous golf courses and tennis courts.

The Phantom Owner of Baynard Plantation

In 1776, Captain John Stoney bought a thousand-acre farm, known as Braddock's Point Plantation, on Hilton Head Island. The main house was constructed with tabby, a common Low Country building material consisting of sand, shells, and lime. The slaves who worked on the plantation lived a mile away from the main house in small cabins in an area known as slave row. Following Stoney's death in 1821, the plantation was passed down to his son, Captain James Stoney. In 1838, James Stoney's son, "Saucy" Jack Stoney, inherited the property. According to one legend, Saucy Jack lost the title to the plantation in a poker game to William Eddings Baynard. In a less scandalous version of the story, Baynard acquired the property after Saucy Jack went bankrupt.

Baynard transformed the plantation into a very profitable enterprise by planting Sea Island cotton, a new cotton hybrid that was extremely popular. Baynard, his wife Catherine, and their four children spent the happiest years of their lives on the plantation. Their familial bliss came to an end in 1849 when Baynard died of yellow fever and was interred at the family tomb in Zion Cemetery. The family left their once happy home just before General William Tecumseh Sherman's Union forces invaded the island. The mansion was occupied by Union troops until Confederate raiders set fire to it. The Baynard family continued to own the property after the Civil War, but they never returned to it. If the legend can be believed, though, one disgruntled family member is still there.

According to one legend, William Baynard's ghost is an active presence on the island because the Federal injunction against desecrating burial sites was not followed during the plantation's occupation. Locals say that the Yankees who took over Hilton Head in 1861 ransacked Baynard's mausoleum while searching for treasure. Baynard's corpse disappeared during the break-in at his tomb and was never recovered. It is said that occasionally his spirit can be seen leading a funeral procession, composed of ghostly mourners and servants, from his home to his mausoleum. Eyewitnesses say that Baynard's ghost gives them the evil eye as he passes by.

A second legend involving Baynard's restless spirit contradicts history. Some people say that William never recovered from the death of his young bride in 1830. On stormy nights, Baynard's despondent spirit is said to drive his wife's hearse, drawn by four black horses. The phantom carriage stops long enough at each former plantation along the way for Baynard to walk up to each gate. The problem with this myth is that his wife did not succumb to yellow fever in 1830.

An unhappy female spirit is also said to haunt the plantation. Supposedly, Baynard's mistress, Eliza, attempted to poison Caroline Baynard. Eliza was hanged from a large oak tree at the intersection of Marshlands Road and Matthews Drive. After she died, her corpse was placed in a metal cage and suspended from the tree as an object lesson. To this day, Eliza's ghost hovers around the "Eliza Tree."

Little remains of the Stoney-Baynard home aside from a slave kitchen, a large tabby stone, and the large, square holes where beams once supported a sizeable porch. Trees now grow on the land where cotton grew more than one hundred and fifty years ago. All vestiges of fine living have vanished. Only the stories of William Eddings Baynard's mournful spirit remain.

The Blue Lady of Hilton Head Island

Female spirits are fairly selective about what they wear in the afterlife, just as they were when they were alive. Most female spirits wear white; a large number also walk around dressed in gray. Only a few female ghosts wear blue. For example, the Vale End Cemetery in New Hampshire is haunted by the ghost of Mary Ritter Spaulding, whose spirit takes the form of a pale blue column of light. The Blue Lady who haunts the Story Inn Restaurant in Brown County, Indiana, is summoned by turning on a blue light in one of the rooms. The Blue Lady, who appears to customers at the Moss Beach Distillery in Moss Beach, California, is the ghost of a young married woman who fell in love with a piano player and was murdered by her husband. On Hilton Head Island, the Blue Lady is said to be the dutiful spirit of the daughter of a lighthouse keeper.

The source of the legend of the Blue Lady of Hilton Head Island can be traced back to a hurricane that landed on the island in August 1898. The gales were so strong that they blew out several windows in the island's lighthouse and extinguished the light. The lighthouse keeper, Adam Fripp, and his young daughter, Caroline, were trying to ignite the light with a torch when suddenly, he clutched his chest and collapsed. Caroline stayed with him in the lighthouse until the next morning. While her father was resting, Caroline kept the light lit through the entire storm. The next morning, she helped her father walk back to the lighthouse keeper's cottage, but Adam Fripp died the following day. Caroline never recovered from the shock of losing her father. She began walking slowly between the lighthouse keeper's cottage and the lighthouse. Onlookers said that she always wore a blue dress. Several weeks after the death of her father, Caroline herself died. For many years, locals claimed to have seen Caroline's ghost standing in front of one of the windows of the lighthouse. They also said that weeping could be heard occasionally coming from the lighthouse keeper's cottage. Sightings of the Blue Lady almost always occur during hurricane season.

Some people believe that Caroline's ghost moved to Harbour Town when Charles Fraser moved the lighthouse keeper's cottage there from the Leamington area of Palmetto Dunes in 1967. At the time, Harbour Town was undergoing its first phases of construction. At night, teenagers would drive out to the remote area on the unpaved sand roads to talk and make out. One night, a young couple drove out on the road leading to the lighthouse keeper's house to park. After a few minutes, a lady dressed in a shimmering blue dress appeared in front of their car. Terrified, the couple sped away as fast as they could. When they returned home, they told their parents about the ghost. Their parents listened patiently and then informed the girl and the boy that they would drive out to the old lighthouse keeper's house to check their story. The four skeptical adults parked in the same spot where their children had seen the Blue Lady and waited. Within a few minutes, they saw a glowing blue shape standing in front of one of the windows of the house. The specter then floated over to the door and hovered over the front porch. The adults stared in awe until the ghost dissipated.

Today, the lighthouse keeper's house is the Harbour Town Bakery and Café, next door to CQ's Restaurant. Some employees at CQ's believe that Caroline's ghost has taken up residence there after leaving the café next door. In an article titled "Our Night with the Blue Lady," author Tom Bastek reports that several years ago, the pay phone at the bakery would ring one short ring every night. When one of the employees picked up the phone, the line would be dead. The manager put up with these interruptions for a while. Finally, he had the pay phone removed. On another occasion, one of the chefs had turned off everything in the restaurant and was preparing to lock up when he realized that he had left something in the kitchen. When he walked into the kitchen, he was surprised to find that one of the burners on the stove was on. He was certain that he had turned the stove off just a few minutes before. A few months later, two wine bottles fell off the shelf upstairs but did not break. The Blue Lady is said to be a mischievous ghost who hides socks and spills cherry juice on the floor during the night.

The story of the Blue Lady is most likely a hybrid of several local legends that have blended together. Who is to say that the active presence in CQ's Restaurant is actually the ghost of Caroline Fripp? One can be sure, though, that the sad story of Caroline Fripp will continue to survive and evolve because it memorializes one girl's selfless devotion to her father and to the lighthouse.

Beware of the Boo Hag!

Early in the eighteenth century, planters living along the Atlantic coast of South Carolina discovered that rice could be grown in the semitropical regions of the state. In order to make their dream a reality, they imported slaves from the rice-growing region of West Africa, stretching from Senegal down to Sierra Leone and Liberia. For the next hundred years, the largest number of slaves brought over to South Carolina from Africa came from the Rice Coast. Descendants of these slaves, the Gullah, can be found all along the coast of South Carolina. The English-based Creole language spoken by these people is peppered with words and phrases that are still spoken by the people of Sierra Leone, such as "pantap" (on top of), "tif" (steal), and "swit" (delicious). The high concentration of slaves from Sierra Leone has left behind a wealth of folklore that is unique to the coastal region of South Carolina. One of the most frightening of the Gullah legends that is still told in places like St. Helena Island is the story of the Boo Hag.

The Boo Hag is a vampire-like creature that sucks the life from human beings. The Boo Hag is blood-red in color because it has no skin. In order to fit in with real people, the Boo Hag often steals the skin from previous victims and continues to wear the skin until it wears out. Before the Boo Hag flies off in search of victims, it hides its purloined skin so that it can use it later. Once the Boo Hag has selected a victim, it enters that person's house at night through a small crack or keyhole while the person is asleep. The Boo Hag then positions itself over its sleeping victim and, in a process known as "ridin'," steals its victim's breath while filling the person's head with peaceful dreams. The next morning, the person feels tired and perhaps short of breath, but for the most part, is left unharmed. Chances are good that the Boo Hag will make repeated visits to its victim's bedroom as long as the person remains asleep. The victim

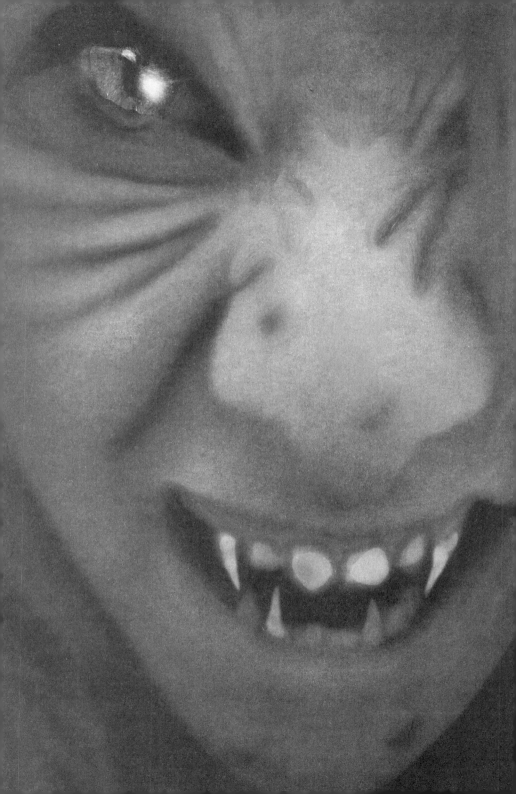

is in no immediate danger unless he or she resists; then the Boo Hag removes the person's skin and flies off into the night. To this day, young people are instructed by their parents and grandparents to keep a broom by their bedside. If the Boo Hag appears in the children's bedroom at night, it will be compelled to count the straws in the broom until sunrise.

The Gullah culture is eroding in South Carolina, as the isolation that helped preserve their traditions for three centuries is slowly being assaulted by the prevailing culture. Coastal development and the need to leave the coast in search of employment are threatening the ancient customs that defined the culture. However, until the Gullah culture disappears completely in South Carolina, old people will continue to tell small children, "Don't let the Boo Hag ride ya!" as they tuck them into bed.

The Summerville Light

Summerville, a distant suburb of Charleston, is a thriving city whose success is due at least in part to its attempt to reach out to tourists. Summerville's annual Flowertown Festival is the largest arts and crafts festival in South Carolina. Downtown Summerville is known for its quilt shop and its drug store, which is the oldest pharmacy in the state with a real soda fountain. One of Summerville's biggest attractions is HollyFest, a weekend Christmas celebration that attracts thousands of visitors with its Christmas parade. Summersville's Christmas Tree Lighting is also a big draw for the town. However, the teenagers who drive out to the railroad tracks on the edge of town are looking for an entirely different type of illumination—one known as the Summerville Light.

One of the legends behind the Summerville Light takes place in the late nineteenth century. Every night at midnight, a woman waited by the railroad tracks for her husband, a night conductor for the Summerville Railroad Company. Holding a lantern in her hand, she gave him his lunch and talked to him while he ate. One night, the conductor did not show up at his appointed time. The next morning, the authorities told the distraught woman that her husband's train had derailed the night before and he was decapitated. The shocking news of her husband's grisly death unhinged the poor woman's mind. Every midnight after the accident, she continued to stand by the railroad tracks with a lunch bucket and her lantern, waiting for her husband, until the day she died.

A second version of the legend, which also takes place in the late 1800s, is told by teenage curiosity-seekers in Summerville. Every night, a man stood by the railroad tracks, lantern in hand, waiting for the train. One night, when the train was late, the man became impatient. He knelt down and laid his head on the rails, hoping to hear the vibrations of the train as it rumbled down the tracks. After a few minutes, the man fell asleep. Suddenly, the man was awakened by shrieking of the train whistle. Unfortunately, he did not lift up his head from the rail in time. His head was severed from his body and rolled down the embankment into the darkness below. Every night, the man's headless corpse wanders around the railroad tracks, swinging his lantern, as he searches for his head.

For decades, young people intrigued by the legends have driven to the same place by the railroad tracks, hoping to see the Summerville Light. Eyewitnesses describe it as a green, glowing ball, similar in color to the light produced by a chemical light stick. People who have seen the light at midnight claim that the entire area became eerily silent when the shining orb appeared. The Summerville Light has been sighted on at least two occasions on Sheep Island Road. In both cases, the cars were parked alongside the road when the shimmering light appeared. A few seconds after the drivers turned the ignition key, the engine stalled. A few tense minutes later, the drivers were able to start their cars. When they drove away, the light pursued them for a mile or so and then vanished.

To view the Summerville Light, drive on Interstate 26 heading toward Summerville. Take Exit 199A and drive 0.2 miles down Highway 17. Take a right onto Berkeley Circle and drive 0.8 miles. Make a right turn onto Sheep Island Road. Drive a mile past a subdivision on the left. Stop at the "End of Maintenance" sign and park in front of a large mound of dirt. Turn off your engine and wait. If you stare over the dirt mound through the woods, and you are very lucky, you might catch a glimpse of the elusive Summerville Light.

The Door That Refused to Stay Closed

Presbyterians first congregated on Edisto Island around 1689. However, the first church building was not constructed until 1710. After the church burned, it was replaced by a new structure in 1807. In 1836, construction of the present Presbyterian Church was completed. Designed by Charleston architect James Curtis, the classic Greek Revival church symbolized the prosperity of the planters who worshipped there. The wooden benches that can still be seen in the old church were used by slaves, who were encouraged to attend services. In the graveyard attached to the church, one can find graves dating back to 1792. The air of melancholy that hangs over the graveyard seemingly emanates from the small, temple-like mausoleum without any doors.

In 1850, a young girl named Julia Legare was staying in the home of her relatives when she developed a yellowish-gray membrane on her throat. She also developed a fever and had difficulty breathing and swallowing. The doctor, who immediately recognized the symptoms of diphtheria, recommended at least ten days of bed rest. Within a few days, the child slipped into a deep coma. Convinced that the girl was dead, the family quickly dressed her lifeless body in her favorite pink dress and interred her that afternoon, hoping to prevent the spread of the disease that had taken hundreds of lives on the state's barrier islands. She was laid to rest in a marble mausoleum with the name "J. B. Legare" carved above the door.

Fifteen years after Julia's death, a coffin containing the corpse of a young man who was killed in an accident was carried to the Legare mausoleum in the Edisto Presbyterian Church Cemetery. When the door to the mausoleum was opened, the mourners were shocked to find the corpse of a little girl in a tattered pink dress lying by the door. Suddenly, it dawned on them that Julia Legare must have been buried alive. They could picture the poor girl climbing out of her coffin and frantically trying to find a way out of her marble prison before dying of starvation. The men sadly gathered up Julia's remains and placed them in her coffin.

In her book *More Tales of the South Carolina Low Country*, Nancy Rhyne relates the conclusion of the horrific tale of Julia

Legare. A few weeks after the funeral of the young man, a family member who had returned to the cemetery was surprised to find the marble door to the mausoleum standing wide open. After locking the door even more securely than it had been before, the man left. A month later, he was surprised to learn from an elder of the church that the door was open once again. For the next one hundred years, all efforts to keep the door to the Legare mausoleum closed failed. In the 1950s, state-of-the-art locks were placed on the door. A few days later, the door was found lying on the ground. The door was placed back on its hinges and locked with a heavy iron chain in a last-ditch effort to keep it closed, but a week later, the door was on the ground. Today, the marble door has been cemented to the floor of the mausoleum.

Even though the door no longer moves on its own, paranormal activity has still been observed in and around the mausoleum. Visitors have captured a number of strange images with their digital cameras, including the pictures of what seem to be angelic and demonic faces. The figure of a young girl in a long dress has also appeared in photographs.

Regrettably, before embalming became widely practiced in the twentieth century, premature burials were not uncommon. In 1674, a sexton who was exhuming the body of Marjorie Halcrow Ersking of Chirnside, Scotland, accidentally revived her while attempting to cut a valuable ring off her finger. In 1896, T. M. Montgomery, who was supervising the disinterring and removal of corpses from Fort Randall Cemetery in South Dakota noticed that 2 percent of all the bodies he removed had been buried alive. Without a doubt, though, one of the most terrible cases of live burial has to be the story of young Julia Legare.

The Melancholy Return of Mary Fickling

One of Edisto Island's most enduring legends is the tragic tale of John Fickling and Mary Clark, who lived in Edingsville on Edisto Island in the first half of the nineteenth century. Because the wealthy planters who owned beach houses at Edisto Island circulated in a very exclusive society, the Fickling and Clark families became very close. John and Mary became inseparable, almost from they day they could walk. They played together as children, collecting seashells and frolicking in the surf. When they entered adolescence, their affection for each other developed into a full-fledged romance. John eventually became a sea captain, and the time they spent apart only intensified their ardor. The announcement of their engagement came as a surprise to no one on the island. Their wedding was a lavish affair. Following John and Mary's marriage in St. Stephen's Church, their guests were treated to a sumptuous banquet on the beach. They feasted on palmetto hearts, turkey, hard-boiled eggs, pound cake, and salad drenched in vinegar dressing.

Mary's love for her husband was so strong that she grew to resent the profession that took John away from her for weeks at a time. A month after they were married, John's ship embarked on a voyage to the West Indies. Inside the hold of the ship was wood and cotton. As she stood on the dock, waving goodbye, Mary was filled with a sense of dread. Her friends and relatives tried to tell her that the three-month voyage would be over before she knew it, but Mary was certain that she would never again see her husband. To her dismay, John's ship did not return on its scheduled arrival date. For the next few days, Mary walked along the shoreline just before sunset, gazing out into the ocean for any sign of John's ship. On October 12, Mary could tell by the churning waves that a large storm was brewing. She rushed home to find that her parents were also concerned about the dark clouds and the choppy sea. All of a sudden, huge waves pummeled the house. Water cascaded through the windows, forcing Mary and her parents to climb on top of the furniture. During the night, they huddled together and prayed while the wind howled around the eaves and the raindrops rattled on the roof.

The next morning, Mary walked out the front door, bolstered by the feeling that this was the day when she would finally be reunited with her husband. As she walked around the debris that littered the beach, she looked intently for any sign of her husband. After a few minutes, her attention was diverted by a white form bobbing in the tide. As she waded into the water, she recognized the form as the body of a man. With trembling hands, she turned the body over. She screamed as she realized that she was staring into the dead face of her husband. Later on, she learned that John's ship was sunk in the hurricane and that all hands were lost.

Today, very little remains of nineteenth-century resort life on Edisto Island. Tourists are drawn to the island by its seafood restaurants, nature trails, beach walks, cottages, and condominiums. However, locals say that one element of the past returns whenever a hurricane strikes Edisto Island. For almost two hundred years, people standing on the beach the day after a hurricane raged through the island have seen the mournful spirit of a young woman dragging the body of a man out of the water onto the beach. Eyewitnesses have stared in wonder as the weeping girl cradles the body of her beloved in her arms before vanishing.

Upstate South Carolina

Most of upstate South Carolina falls within a geographical region called the Piedmont. Consisting primarily of an eroded mountain range, the Piedmont is a very hilly, rocky region that is unsuitable for farming. At one time, mills were built on the fall line, where rivers cascade from higher to lower elevations on the eastern edge of the Piedmont. The availability of water power made the Piedmont an important manufacturing center.

In the extreme northwestern part of the state lies a region called the Blue Ridge. This region contains a portion of the Blue Ridge Mountains. The highest point in South Carolina, Sassafras Mountain, can be found in this area. All of the mountains in the Blue Ridge region are heavily forested. Forming part of the border between South Carolina and Georgia is the Chattooga River, which attracts whitewater rafters from around the nation.

The Ghost Hound of Goshen

Ghost dogs have been a staple of ghost stories for centuries. The most famous ghost dog is, of course, the Hound of the Baskervilles. However, spectral canines can also be found in Southern folklore. For more than a century, travelers making their way down the lonely back roads of Surgoinsville, Tennessee, found their wagons

accompanied by the spirit of the "Long Dog," an oddly shaped white dog that was killed, along with its owners, by the outlaw John Murrell in the 1830s. In Mentone, Alabama, locals still tell the story of the faithful Great Dane, Looksee, who haunts the site of the cabin of his former owner, Granny Dollar, on Lookout Mountain. The best-known ghost dog in South Carolina is the Hound of Goshen, which is said to appear in Newberry County.

The Hound of Goshen has been haunting Maybinton Road for more than a century and a half. In the first half of the nineteenth century, Maybinton Road, which was known as Old Bascombe Road, was originally part of a stagecoach route from Columbia to North Carolina. Today, Maybinton Road runs parallel to Interstate 26. In the early 1850s, a peddler and his faithful dog were passing through a small village on Old Bascombe Road called Goshen Township. According to one version of the tale, the peddler had swindled some of the residents of Goshen out of their hard-earned goods. His nefarious activities attracted the attention of a couple rascals who sneaked up to the wooded spot where the peddler was sleeping and beat him senseless before making off with their booty. The peddler's dog crept up to his master's motionless body and began to howl. The dog's whining attracted the attention of Dr. George Douglas, who lived nearby. The doctor tried to nurse the peddler back to health, but he succumbed to his injuries within a few hours. The peddler was interred in a potter's field not far from where he was murdered. His faithful hound lay down on his master's grave and refused to leave, despite the best efforts of Dr. Douglas and others to lure him away. The poor animal eventually died of exposure and starvation.

In another version of the story, the peddler was walking through Goshen when he was erroneously identified as the murderer of a local man. After a speedy trial, the peddler, who had no one to speak in his defense, was hanged. The peddler's dog remained by the hanging tree until his master's body was cut down and buried. The canine lay down on his master's grave for three days until it was finally stoned to death by locals. In the 1880s, an old man lying on his deathbed confessed to the murder and proved the innocence of the unfortunate peddler.

In both versions of the story, people traveling on Old Bascombe Road reported seeing a large white dog that followed their wagons.

Some people were so annoyed by the dog that they tried to drive it away by shouting at it or lashing it with their buggy whips, but the canine always kept up its relentless pace until they reached Evans Cemetery by the Ebenezer Methodist Church near Newberry. They said that the dog ran up to the cemetery gates and dematerialized as it passed through them. Dr. Douglas said that he formed a sort of bond with the ghost dog, which frequently accompanied him on his rounds. In his later years, Dr. Douglas recalled a visit from a little slave boy. In a trembling voice, the boy said that he was riding a mule down Old Bascombe Road when a large white dog emerged from the gates of the Evans graveyard and began following him. All of a sudden, the dog ran in front of the mule, causing him to rear up. Somehow, the boy avoided tumbling off the mule, and they continued down the road as fast as the mule could go.

Sightings of the Hound of Goshen continued well into the twentieth century after Old Bascombe Road had been paved. In 1936, a teenage boy named Barry Sanders was walking home through Goshen one night when he looked over his shoulder and noticed a large white dog loping behind him. When the boy realized that there was something wrong with the dog, he started running. By the time he reached Dr. Douglas's former house, the young man was so winded that he nearly passed out from exhaustion. In the late 1970s, an elderly woman was sitting on her porch late one evening when she noticed a large white dog bounding down the sidewalk directly toward her. Just before the dog reached the porch, the woman fainted. When she regained consciousness, the dog was gone.

The Musical Ghosts of Sullivan Hall

Anderson College in Anderson was founded as a Baptist women's college in 1847 by Reverend William B. Johnson. The school was forced to close during the Civil War, and it stayed shuttered for decades. However, in 1910, a group of citizens interested in bringing higher education back to Anderson offered thirty acres of land and $100,000 to the South Carolina Baptist Convention in hopes of enticing them to reopen the school. The South Carolina General Assembly granted the college a charter in 1911, and Anderson College reopened its doors in 1912 as a four-year college for women. Anderson College became coeducational in 1930. On January 1,

2006, Anderson College became Anderson University. Today, Anderson University is ranked in the top tier of Southern Comprehensive Universities by *U.S. News and World Report*. Anderson University has also gained recognition for the ghost that may or may not haunt Sullivan Hall.

Sullivan Hall was originally the President's Mansion at the university. According to campus lore, Anna, the daughter of one of the former presidents, fell in love with a handsome young man named Francis. Anna's father disapproved of the match because she was only sixteen years old. Francis was several years older and Catholic as well. One day, Anna informed her father that she and Francis had gotten engaged, in spite of his disapproval. His face flush with anger, Anna's father told her that he was not going to allow his daughter to marry someone like Francis. Sobbing, Anna marched upstairs and hanged herself.

Rumors of ghostly activity in the old building circulated around the Anderson campus for years. By the 1980s, the President's Mansion had been converted into the Sullivan Music Center. Several reports of paranormal activity inside the center were included in an article published in the December 19, 1982, issue of the *Anderson Independent Mail*. Several maintenance workers told the reporter that early one morning in December 1982, they had heard singing and someone playing the piano. Two other maintenance workers, Ernie Edwards and Donnie Martin, said that they were cleaning the ground floor when they heard music coming from the back of the building. As Edwards and Martin cautiously walked toward the sound, they realized that the music was getting louder. Finally, the two men turned around and left the building because Edwards' heart "couldn't take it." The director of the physical plant added that he heard someone walking on the steps of the Sullivan Music Center one morning before dawn. After that experience, he swore that no one would ever "catch [him] in that music building before daylight."

Not everyone connected with Anderson University agrees that Sullivan Music Center is haunted, however. In her book *South Carolina Ghosts: From the Coast to the Mountains*, author Nancy Roberts says that the maintenance men are no longer willing to discuss the strange occurrences in the Sullivan Music Center. According to the administration at the university, no records exist of any president's daughter having committed suicide. Roberts quotes Paul Talmadge, an academic dean, who said, "Nothing tragic has ever happened on this campus or in the music building." In the 1990s, after the building was renovated to house the offices for campus ministries, rumors of haunted activity in the former music center persisted. Greg Allgood, director of Anderson University campus ministries, heard about the strange sounds in the building before he moved in, but he did not take the stories very seriously. "I've had students say they heard things late at night, but I mostly attribute that to this being an old house," Allgood said.

The Belmont Inn

The Belmont Inn had its inception in the mind of Philip Rosenburg and a number of other prominent citizens of Abbeville in 1901. The contract for the construction of the hotel was awarded to an Atlanta firm, who agreed to build it for the then-extravagant cost of $25,000. When the Eureka Hotel, as it was known at the time, had its grand opening on April 29, 1903, it was one of the finest hotels in northwest South Carolina. The local newspaper awed its readers with its descriptions of the new hotel's amenities, including barber shops, baths, parlors, offices, sitting rooms, dining rooms, and luxurious bedrooms. The Eureka's clientele consisted mostly of performers at the Abbeville Opera House and businessmen who arrived by train. Beginning in the 1950s, the hotel experienced a period of decline, which continued until it finally closed in 1972. The hotel was renovated in the early 1980s and reopened on November 23, 1984, under a new name, the Belmont Inn.

In her book *Ghosts of the South Carolina Midland*, Tally Johnson says that the Belmont Inn is haunted by two male ghosts. One of these ghosts, known to the staff as Abraham, is usually seen on the ground floor. Staff and guests have rarely caught more than just a fleeting glimpse of this elusive spirit. Another ghost, identified as "the Scotsman," manifests himself only on the main stairs. Guests have been awakened by the sound of a ghostly knocking on their doors. Members of the staff complain that small objects occasionally turn up missing for a while but then reappear in different locations. In addition, glasses have been knocked off tables by unseen hands.

The most active part of the Belmont Inn is Rooms 10 and 12. Members of the staff say that a decorative bust has been known to turn around on its own. A guest who stayed in Room 12 claimed to have seen a full-bodied apparition standing by the bed. Cold spots have also been detected in Room 12.

An investigation of the ghostly activity at the Belmont Inn was conducted by a ghost-hunting group named East Georgia Paranormal. Investigators spent two nights in Rooms 10 and 12. The first night of the investigation, team members marked the position of the bust; at the end of the second day, the bust appeared to have rotated ten degrees off the mark. The second night, a couple staying at the hotel asked investigators to check out the voices they had been hearing. Using a nightshot camera, the team captured a shadow in the dark room. The most disturbing personal experience of the entire investigation occurred when an investigator standing in the hotel elevator felt an invisible hand touch his back.

Today, the Belmont Inn boasts twenty-five newly remodeled rooms and the Heritage Dining Room and the Belmont Tavern. Corporate meetings, seminars, wedding receptions, and family reunions are held at the inn. Apparently, most guests are not deterred by the prospect of having their stay interrupted by the occasional appearance of Abraham or the Scotsman.

The Vigilant Spirit of the South Carolina School for the Deaf and Blind

In 1849, the Reverend Newton Pinckney Walker and his wife, Martha Hughston Walker, founded the Cedar Springs Asylum. The first class consisted of five students, three of whom were Mrs. Walker's siblings. In 1855, Reverend Walker hired James S. Henderson to teach blind students who had been admitted to the school. The school's name changed to the South Carolina Institution for the Education of the Deaf and Dumb and Blind in 1856 when it was purchased by the State of South Carolina for $10,759. In 1860, construction of the main building was completed. In 1861, Martha Walker took over management of the school. The school was closed briefly after the Civil War but reopened in 1869 with a superintendent, John M. Hughston, who was the school's first graduate. In

1995, the name of the main building was changed to honor Martha Walker. Even though the Walkers no longer run the South Carolina School for the Deaf and Blind, students say that the spirit of Martha is still patrolling the halls.

Most of the sightings of Martha Walker have occurred in the museum in Walker Hall. In the book *Ghosts of the South Carolina Upcountry*, Tally Johnson tells the story of a graduate student who saw the ghost in 1980. He was sorting photographs on the second floor when he thought he saw someone out in the hallway. Thinking that he was alone, he stepped outside the door of the office and saw a woman whose face resembled that of Martha Walker. Within seconds, the woman vanished.

In the early 2000s, a security guard had an unnerving experience on the third floor of Walker Hall. He was making his nightly rounds when he decided to check out one of the offices. He turned on the light and was shocked to see a swivel chair turning around on its own. Sensing that he was in the presence of something otherworldly, the security guard ran out of the office and exited the building. He remained outside the building for the rest of the night.

Many people have had uneasy feelings on the third floor of Walker Hall. Some students have reported seeing moving shadows in the hallway. Others have had the uneasy feeling that someone—or something—is watching them on the third floor. With the exception of a seeing-eye dog that inexplicably raised its hackles in a third-floor office, very few people have felt threatened by the spirit that has made Walker Hall its home. The students, faculty, and administrators who have seen Mrs. Walker's ghost have gotten the impression that she is a protective spirit who continues to look after the students in her school.

Hell's Gate Cemetery

In communities throughout the South, many of the region's legends have been transmitted by people in their teens and their twenties. In Spartanburg, one of the most popular teen hot spots is an old cemetery they call "Hell's Gate Cemetery." The actual name of the cemetery is Oakwood Cemetery. It is located off East Main Street and Oakwood Street, close to Converse College. The oldest cemetery in Spartanburg, Oakwood Cemetery is the final resting place for a number of politicians, such as Joseph Travis Johnson (1859–1919), who served as U.S. Representative from South Carolina and U.S. District Judge for the Western District of South Carolina. John Adam Henneman (1835–91), a judge who was assassinated by John Williams on September 27, 1891, is also buried here. Spartanburg's most impoverished residents are buried in a potter's field down a hill in the back of the cemetery. However, the young people who park here at night are not interested in the history that lies under their feet. They are hoping to catch a glimpse of the ghosts that are said to wander the cemetery.

Many people have had strange experiences in Oakwood Cemetery over the years. It is said that cell phones and cameras do not work in the oldest section of the cemetery. Strange lights flutter through the woods surrounding the graveyard. Cold spots are said to exist in certain parts of the cemetery. White mists and orbs have been captured in photographs and posted on the Internet. Some visitors have gone away with the unsettling feeling that they were being watched by someone who could not be seen.

The most active part of the cemetery seems to be the children's burial area. Visitors have heard ghostly voices and laughter of children in this part of the cemetery. Some people claim to have seen spectral children running around the tombstones. The most active little spirit in this part of the cemetery is the ghost of a little boy who is said to have fallen off a cliff while playing with a ball. A number of young people have sworn that the child's ghost walked up to them and asked them to play ball with him. In 2004, a woman walking through this section heard faint singing coming from a particular grave. When her husband took her picture, an orb could clearly be seen hovering over the tombstone.

Even though the ghostly activity at Oakwood Cemetery has sent chills down the spines of hundreds of visitors, the most frightening denizens of the cemetery are human. Oakwood Cemetery is said to be a dangerous place to visit after dark because of the "bad" people who hang around there. Satanists have been said to perform dark rituals in the cemetery at midnight. One young man who tried to enter the cemetery after dark said that the scariest entity he encountered was the caretaker, who told him to go home.

The Inn at Meridun

The house that is known today as The Inn at Meridun was built in 1855–57 by a local merchant named William Keenan. The house and property, which originally included four thousand acres, was known as Keenan Plantation. In 1876, Benjamin H. Rice, a local lawyer from Union, purchased Keenan Plantation so that he could combine it with an adjoining plantation, Pleasant Grove. At the time, the combined eight-thousand-acre cotton plantation was among the most productive in the northern part of the state. In 1885, the grandson of Benjamin H. Rice, Thomas Cary Duncan, inherited the plantation house, which had been extensively renovated several years before. Duncan combined three family names—Meriman, Rice, and Duncan—and renamed the house Meridun. Seven generations of the Benjamin Rice family lived continuously on the plantation for 114 years. Then in 1990, Jim and Peg Waller purchased the home for the purpose of converting it into a bed and breakfast. The Wallers immediately began remodeling the house. After the house was completely renovated, it opened in 1992 under the name "The Inn at Meridun." It was not long before it became apparent that the remodeling of the old house might have stirred up a number of spirits.

According to a clairvoyant who visited the inn, at least ten ghosts are said to haunt The Inn at Meridun. In her book *Haunted Inns of the Southeast*, author Sheila Turnage said that Peg Waller's brother saw the ghost of a short, buxom woman in a blue-gray dress. Peg believes that she is the spirit of Mary Wallace, the spinster sister of one of the previous owners of the house. Several female guests have reported being touched by a male spirit during the night. Peg's husband has encountered the ghost of a red-headed woman who has called his name in the middle of the night.

Ghostly activity that cannot be attributed to a specific person has also been reported at the inn. The Wallers' cat, J. D., seems to be particularly sensitive to one of the spirits, possibly that of a little white dog that has been known to jump on beds and growl at guests. Harpsichord music occasionally wafts through the rooms and hallways. People have detected the smell of cigar smoke and perfume in some of the rooms. In the guest book, a few guests have reported hearing the voices of a man and a woman. One guest heard the laughter of women in an empty room. Another guest heard a male voice saying, "Be careful." Some guests have had their camera batteries depleted inside the inn. Ghost hunters have captured orbs, swirling mists, and EVPs inside the hotel. Guests have also seen the ghost of an African-American housekeeper performing her chores in the inn.

Of course, The Inn at Meridun has much more to offer guests than the opportunity to have a paranormal experience. The floor plan includes seven bedrooms, a music room, a parlor, and a library. The inn's lavish furnishings include beautiful chandeliers, frescoed ceilings in the music room and dining room, and mosaic tiles in the main foyer. Nevertheless, the appearance of The Inn at Meridun on at least one listing of the ten most haunted bed-and-breakfasts in the United States has definitely not been bad for business.

Foster's Tavern

In 1801, Anthony Foster began building a tavern at the intersection of the old Pickneyville and Georgia roads. Seven years later, Foster's Tavern was open for business. Built with bricks handmade in the area, the walls of the tavern are between eighteen inches and thirty-six inches thick. To make his tavern more appealing to the eye, Foster built a second-floor balcony, a pedimented entrance portico with fanlight, and American Gothic chimneys at each end of the gabled roof. Inside the tavern, guests marveled at the hand-carved woodwork, including fluted door casings, eight mantels, paneled wainscoting in two rooms, and scrollwork on stair stringers. In 1845, the owners added the entrance portico. The porches were constructed in 1915.

In the early nineteenth century, Foster's Tavern was one of the finest hostels in northern South Carolina. John C. Calhoun, a frequent guest at the tavern, always stayed in the southwest corner room on the second floor during his travels between Fort Hill and Columbia. In 1810, Bishop Francis Asbury, the founder of Methodism in South Carolina, stopped at Foster's Tavern. The lingering presence of these long-dead visitors at Foster's Tavern has been the subject of ghost stories in the area for more than one hundred years.

People living in the area began telling stories about the haunting of Foster's Tavern around the turn of the twentieth century. Residents have heard voices and footsteps in the middle of the night. Tally Johnson, author of *Ghosts of the South Carolina Upcountry*, reports seeing the transparent image of a woman standing just inside the glass panel of one of the doors. One of the owners was giving piano lessons when she saw a skeletal hand reach through the back door. Her terror escalated when she realized that an old family cemetery was in the backyard. The oddest activity in the house is the frequently reported sound of horses' hooves on the roof.

Some people believe that most of the paranormal activity in Foster's Tavern is caused by the restless spirit of a boarder who hanged himself in the garret. This theory is substantiated by the fact that several people have heard sinister voices coming from the attic. It is also possible that this mournful spirit produced the moaning sounds that were recorded inside the house. However, eyewitness accounts suggest that this spirit is not the only ghost haunting the now privately owned residence—just the noisiest.

The Devil's Castle

The Greenville County Tuberculosis Hospital began admitting patients on July 29, 1930. For more than two decades, hundreds of people were treated for night sweats, fever, tiredness, breathlessness, and chest pain. In the late 1950s, the hospital was abandoned. In 1974, the building was converted into a work-release center for prisoners. Twenty-three years later, the center was closed, and the building stood abandoned once again while the state looked into adapting it for another use. In 2002, a group of vagrants who had started a fire to keep warm accidentally set the building ablaze. The county bulldozed the heavily damaged building in 2005. Today, the site of the Greenville County Tuberculosis Hospital is occupied by Herdklotz Park. For many people, though, the misery and suffering of the past has not been entirely covered over by the soccer field, playground, and walking trails.

Many residents of Greenville still remember when the abandoned building, dubbed "the Devil's Castle" by adventurous teenagers, was rumored to be haunted. Some young people reported being pushed from behind while walking on the third floor. It was said that objects moved by themselves in darkened rooms and hallways. According to Terrance Zepke, author of *Best Ghost Tales of South Carolina*, a number of terrified witnesses standing on the driveway said that they saw and heard the shadowy images of people running through the building. Some trespassers also claimed to have heard singing, clanking noises, and the sounds of objects being dragged across the floor. Several people claimed to have heard the sound of footsteps that break into a run, followed by screams, on the first floor.

Apparently, the construction of the park has not removed all of the residual paranormal activity on the site. A number of eerie sounds have been recorded on the playground in recent years. These EVPs include banging sounds, screaming, talking, and the ringing of a bell. At night, bizarre shadows have been seen flitting around the park.

Today, nothing remains of the Greenville County Tuberculosis Hospital except for what is left of the root cellar, a few steps, and scattered fragments of brick and broken glass jotting out of the sod. Signs recount the sad history of a hospital whose staff cared for patients considered outcasts by general society. "The Devil's Castle" also survives in the memories of people who can still recall venturing into the spooky old structure as teenagers in the hope of having an encounter with the supernatural.

The Lizardman of Bishopville

"Lizardman" is a term coined by cryptozoologists to refer to reptilian hominids that walk on two legs. Lizardmen have been sighted all over the world, with names such as the Intulo of South Africa, the Loveland Frogman of Ohio, and the New Jersey Gator Man. In South Carolina, a lizardlike creature has been terrifying the residents of Bishopville since it was first sighted in the swamps in the late 1980s.

The first officially recognized encounter with the creature that came to be known as the Lizardman occurred on June 19, 1988. Seventeen-year-old Christopher Davis was driving along a lonely road near Scape Ore Swamp at 2:00 A.M. when his car suffered a flat tire. Christopher pulled off the road and changed the flat. He had just replaced the tire with the spare and was in the process of placing the jack in the trunk when he heard a strange grunting sound. Christopher stared in the direction of the grunts and was shocked to see a seven-foot-tall, greenish-colored creature running toward him. Christopher slammed the trunk shut, jumped into his car, and drove off. His relief at having escaped his pursuer was short-lived, however. He had not driven very far down the road before he heard a crashing sound on the roof of his car and saw a large, three-fingered hand reach across his windshield. Christopher recalled later that the hand had scales and long, sharp claws. Terrified, Christopher sped up and swerved off the road. As he swerved back onto the road, he was pleased to see that the creature had fallen off his car.

Not long thereafter, Lee County sheriff Liston Truesdale heard about Christopher Davis's encounter with the strange creature. Curious to see if the rumors he had heard about the monster were true, Sheriff Truesdale contacted Christopher and asked him if he would agree to take a lie detector test. As it turned out, Christopher was eager to have his story verified, so he readily agreed to the test. He also drew a picture of the creature he saw in the swamp. The polygraph test was administered by Sumter police captain Earl Berry and paid for by Southern Marketing Incorporated. To the sheriff's surprise, Christopher easily passed the test.

Sheriff Truesdale was reading the results of Davis's exam when he recalled another encounter with a strange beast that was reported to him in June by a thirty-one-year-old construction worker named George Hollomon Jr. Hollomon was riding his bike in the area when he stopped by an artesian well near the Scape Ore Swamp Bridge to drink some water and smoke a cigarette. Hollomon said he was standing by his bike, staring across the road, when he saw something between seven and eight feet tall stand up. As a car passed by, Hollomon noticed that the creature had glowing eyes.

Other eyewitnesses soon came forward in the months that followed Davis's sighting. Brian Edward and Michelle Nunnery told Sheriff Truesdale that they were driving along Cedar Creek Road shortly after midnight when they almost ran over a two-legged beast. Before long, reporters from the *Los Angeles Times*, the *Herald Examiner*, the *Charlotte Observer*, and *Time* magazine descended on Bishopville. Radio station WCOS offered $1 million to anyone who captured the creature. "Lizard mania" in Bishopville peaked when a story on the Lizardman was broadcast on the CBS Evening News. The furor died down after an air force sergeant was found to have dressed up like a giant lizard and walked around the swamp.

The Lizardman resurfaced in the early 1990s. A colonel in the Army Corps of Engineers told the sheriff that he saw a half-man, half-lizard creature as he drove past Scape Ore Swamp. He refused to file a formal report, however, for fear of harming his career. A few months later, the Blathers family was driving through the area on their return home from a fast-food restaurant when they saw a large, hairy creature standing on the road. The Blatherses were so frightened by their experience that they went directly to Sheriff Truesdale's office. The family members were placed in different rooms to see if their stories matched during their interviews. Each person described the beast in the same way.

Reports of the Lizardman ceased until the mid-2000s. In October 2005, a woman who lived in Newberry told police that she had seen two lizardmen standing outside her home. The police dismissed the woman's sighting because she could have been influenced by promotions for the South Carolina Education Lottery that featured the Lizardman. More concrete evidence of the Lizardman's existence came to light in late February 2008. Dixie Rawson, a resident of Bishopville, sent an e-mail to television station WIS News 10 in which she claimed that something had attacked the front of her van. She also noticed that the morning newspaper and the towels inside the cat box had been shredded. Several of the twenty cats that lived on the property mysteriously disappeared. Not long after the attack on Rawson's vehicle, police discovered a dead coyote and a dead cow in a nearby field. However, police ruled out the Lizardman as the culprit because the blood traces from the Dawson van turned out to be coyote blood.

The numerous sightings of the Lizardman over the years have put Lee County on the map, so to speak. The annual Lizard Man 5K Run attracts hundreds of visitors to Bishopville. The chamber of commerce has also exploited its connection with the monster through the sale of "Lizard Man" and "Lizard Patrol" T-shirts. The Bishopville Lizardman even made an appearance on the premiere episode of the Cartoon Network program *The Secret Saturdays* on October 3, 2008. Evidently, there is an upside to having a horrendous, lizard-like creature lurking around.

The Fairfield Witch Trial

The Salem, Massachusetts, witch trials of 1692 immediately come to mind when one thinks of witches in the United States. However, another witch trial on a much smaller scale was held in Fairfield County, South Carolina, a century later in 1792. Philip Edward Pearson, a lawyer from South Carolina, wrote about the trial in 1854 in a manuscript titled "History of Fairfield County, South Carolina." Pearson's manuscript ended up in the library of the Wisconsin Historical Society in Madison, Wisconsin. The manuscript first received national attention through "The Witches of Fairfield South Carolina," an article published by Lee R. Gandee in the January 1970 edition of *FATE* magazine. It revealed that although four people were accused of practicing witchcraft, the star of the trial was a German woman named Mary Ingleman.

In 1792, a number of people were stricken with a strange disease that caused them to act as if they were possessed by the devil. Cattle sickened and died as well. A woman named Rose Henley accused Mary Ingleman, an herbalist and healer, of casting a similar spell on Drury Walker's two children. Ingleman was also accused by her son, Adam Free, of bewitching one of his cows, which jumped up in the air and broke its neck when it landed. Mary's grandson, Jacob Free, swore that Mary turned him into a horse, which she rode to a "grand convention of witches." Isaac Collins claimed that Mary had transformed him into a horse as well.

Mary and three other elderly people were tried in the home of Thomas Hill, five miles south of Winnsboro. Mr. Hill served as a judge during the trial. John Crossland acted as sheriff and executioner. Following testimony by the plaintiffs, the defendants, who did not testify, were found guilty. After they were tied to the joists of the building, the four convicted witches were severely flogged. Later, the soles of their feet were held to a blazing fire and burned.

After her feet recovered sufficiently from the torture, Mary Ingleman began walking back home. She had gone only a short distance from Hill's farm when a man rushed out of the darkness and attacked her. He threw her on the ground and attempted to strangle her by dropping a pine log on her neck. Unable to move because of the heavy log, Mary remained pinned to the ground all night until a kindly stranger happened by the next morning and freed her. After she recovered from her ordeal, Mary went to another judge, Reverend William Youngue; he was the only magistrate in Fairfield County who was willing to issue a warrant for the arrest of John Crossland in the assault on Mary Ingleman. Crossland was found guilty of aggravated assault and fined five pounds. The former sheriff fled west without paying his fine.

Witchcraft faded in Fairfield County after the trial. Perhaps the spectacle of four elderly, respected members of the community having their feet held to the fire was too much for most people to bear. It is also possible that the citizens of Fairfield County became more tolerant of people who did not conform to the norms of society.

Ghosts of Newberry College

Newberry College had its inception in 1828 during a meeting of the Lutheran Synod in South Carolina and Adjacent States. Three years after the president of the synod, the Reverend John Bachman, recommended the establishment of a school for the training of Lutheran ministers, a seminary and classical academy opened its doors near Pomaria. The seminary moved to Newberry in 1856, only one year after it became a degree-granting institution. Newberry College fell on hard times during the Civil War, largely because most of the faculty and students had enlisted in the military. By the end of the war, the only building on campus had been taken over by Union troops. In 1868, the college accepted the offer of St. John's Lutheran Church to move the campus to Walhalla until the main building on the Newberry campus could be restored. Nine years later, the college returned to Newberry, where it has remained ever since. Today, the ninety-acre college offers twenty-one majors and twenty-nine minors. It also offers students fleeting glimpses of the past in the shadowy recesses of its historic buildings.

Like many Southern colleges and universities, Newberry College has a haunted dormitory, Kinard Hall. Apparently, a poltergeist—a mischievous, noisy spirit who creates physical disturbances—is disrupting lives of students living on the second floor. Some say that cabinets and drawers are opened by an unseen hand. Windows open without warning. Faucets turn on by themselves. The identity of the spirit responsible for the activity is unknown.

Newberry College's best-known ghost has a name: Madeline. According to one version of Newberry's oldest legend, Madeline was a young girl who fell in love with one of the Union soldiers who were occupying the campus. When the occupying force was recalled, Madeline became despondent. She took to wandering the campus in a daze, looking for the Yankee soldier who would never return. After time, Madeline's loneliness became intolerable. One evening, she walked inside Keller Hall. Madeline climbed the stairs all the way to the top of the bell tower and stepped off the ledge into the darkness below. For decades, students walking past Keller Hall in the evening have reported seeing the melancholy figure of a woman staring down at them from atop the bell tower. However, Heather Dawkins Stalker, author of "Legendary: A Spine-Tingling Tour," doubts the authenticity of the story. Even though Keller Hall is the second oldest building on campus, it was not built until 1895, thirty years after Federal troops pulled out of Newberry.

Kinard Hall and Keller Hall are not the only allegedly haunted locations on campus. In fact, ghostly activity has been reported throughout the entire school. Windows and doors have been known to open and close by themselves in a number of different buildings. Occasionally, the ghosts of two Confederate soldiers have been seen strolling across the grounds. Newberry College, it seems, cannot escape its past. The past will not allow it.

The Ghostly Convicts of Tillman Hall

David Bancroft Johnson, the superintendent of schools in Columbia, founded Winthrop Training School in 1886. It opened its doors in a one-room building in Columbia. The school moved to its present location in Rock Hill in 1895. The college went through several name changes over the years until becoming Winthrop University—named for Massachusetts philanthropist Robert C. Winthrop—in 1892. Although the University has since expanded the number of majors it offers, its primary mission has not changed since its founding: the training of elementary and secondary teachers. If the stories told by students, faculty, and staff can be believed, some of the people seen about campus have remained unchanged as well, especially at Tillman Hall.

Built in 1894 with convict labor, Tillman Hall is one of the oldest buildings on campus. Remnants of the stockades used to contain the prisoners are still in the basement. The building itself is named after Benjamin Tillman, the governor of South Carolina, who was the keynote speaker when the cornerstone was laid. Tillman was famous for his short temper. In fact, he was called "Pitchfork Ben" because he once threatened to stab President Grover Cleveland with a pitchfork. When he served as a U.S. senator, Tillman was censured for attacking fellow South Carolina senator John L. McLaurin.

Tillman's spirit is assumed to be the ghost that haunts Tillman Hall, probably because it bears his name. However, other ghosts seem to be active in the old building as well. For many years, students have heard the sounds of phantom footsteps walking behind them down empty corridors. Doors have been known to open and close by themselves. Lights flicker on and off for no reason. Cold spots are occasionally detected in certain locations within the building. A shadowy figure has been known to glare at students from the front portico.

The October 4, 2007, edition of *FYE: The News Bulletin for the Winthrop University Community* reported several ghostly encounters in Tillman Hall. Amanda Stewart, who had heard the spectral footsteps and ghostly whispers on different occasions, said that she saw a shadow walk past the doorway of her office one evening when she was working late. Teleia White reported that she was moving paperwork from a coworker's office to the storeroom when she noticed a white card lying on the floor. When she and her coworker examined the card, they were shocked to discover that it was a Christmas card from university founder David Bancroft Johnson. One evening when Debbie Garrick was leaving her office, she had just grabbed the doorknob when she heard the sound of a woman gasping. Later, Debbie said that it sounded like she had surprised someone when she was closing the door.

Because Winthrop University is so picturesque, its campus has been featured in several Hollywood movies. Not surprisingly, one of these films was a horror movie. In 2006, scenes for the direct-to-video movie *Asylum* were filmed in a number of buildings on campus, including Tillman Hall. The film is about a fictional university,

Richard Miller University, where students undergoing freshman orientation are tortured by the ghost of a mad scientist. Although many filmgoers who saw the film when it was released in 2008 said that it was scary, most students agreed that the manufactured chills in the movie could not compare to the real apparitions that haunt Tillman Hall.

Bibliography

Books and Articles

Brunvand, Jan Harold. *The Vanishing Hitchhiker: American Urban Legends & Their Meanings*. New York: W. W. Norton & Company, 1981.

Downer, Deborah L., ed. *Classic American Ghost Stories*. Little Rock, AR: August House, 1990.

Guiley, Rosemary Ellen. *Encyclopedia of Ghosts and Spirits*. New York: Checkmark Books, 2000.

Hauck, Dennis William. *Haunted Places: The National Directory*. New York: Penguin, 1994.

Holzer, Hans. *More Where the Ghosts Are: The Ultimate Guide to Haunted Houses*. New York: Citadel Press, 2002.

Johnson, Tally. *Ghosts of the South Carolina Midlands*. Charleston, SC: The History Press, 2007.

———. *Ghost Stories of the South Carolina Upcountry*. Charleston, SC: The History Press, 2005.

Manley, Roger, Mark Moran, and Mark Sceurman. *Weird Carolinas*: New York: Barnes & Noble Books, 2007.

Ogden, Tom. *The Complete Idiot's Guide to Ghosts and Hauntings*. Indianapolis, IN: Macmillan USA, 1999.

Rhyne, Nancy. *Coastal Ghosts*. Orangeburg, SC: Sandlapper Press, 1985.

Roberts, Nancy. *Haunted Houses: Tales from 30 American Homes*. Chester, CT: Globe Pequot Press, 1988.

———. *South Carolina Ghosts from the Coast to the Mountains*. Columbia, SC: University of South Carolina Press, 1983.

Russell, Lawrence. *Charleston, South Carolina: City under Siege*. Charleston, SC: Charleston Postcard Company, 2000.

Russell, Randy, and Janet Barnett. *Ghost Dogs of the South*. Winston-Salem, NC: John F. Blair, 2001.

Sammons, Mary Beth, and Robert Edwards. *American Hauntings*. New York: Barnes & Noble Books, 2005.

Turnage, Sheila. *Haunted Inns of the Southeast*. Winston-Salem, NC: John F. Blair, 2001.

Online Sources

"A Brief History of St. Philip's Church." Stphilipschurchsc.org. Retrieved 1 January 2009. http://www.stphilipschurchsc.org/spce/history.

"Anderson University (South Carolina)." Wikipedia. Retrieved 21 December 2008. http://en.wikipedia.org/wiki/Anderson_University_(South_Carolina).

"Apelike Monsters: Bigfoot." Unexplainedstuff.com. Retrieved 22 December 2008. http://www.unexplainedstuff.com/Mysterious-Creatures/Apelike-Monsters-Bigfoot.html.

"Archibald Hamilton Rutledge 1883–1973." Sandlapper Publishing, Inc. Retrieved 8 January 2009. http://www.sandlapperpublishing.com/arch.html.

"Asylum." Answers.com. Retrieved 15 January 2009. http://www.answers.com/topic/asylum-2007-film.

Bastek, Tom. "Our Night with the Blue Lady." Celebratehiltonhead.com. Retrieved 18 December 2008. http://www.celebratehiltonhead.com/article/265/our-night-with-the-blue-lady.

"Battery Park in Charleston." Dreamcharleston.com. Retrieved 27 March 2009. http://www.dreamcharleston.com/charleston-battery.html.

"Belmont Hotel: The Hotel." Bobbysuniverse.net. Retrieved 24 January 2009. http://www.bobbysuniverse.net/belmont.htm.

"The Belmont Inn." Belmontinn.net. Retrieved 14 January 2009. http://www.belmontinn.net/?id=6.

"Poogan's Porch Restaurant." Poogansporch.com. Retrieved 4 February 2009. http://www.poogansporch.com/bios.html.

"Boo Hag." Wikipedia. Retrieved 1 January 2009. http://en.wikipedia.org/wiki/Boo_Hag.

Burtinshaw, Julie. "John and Mary." Ghost House Books. Retrieved 30 January 2009. http://www.ghostbooks.net/story.php?id=044.

Butler, Pat. "Bigfoot Expert Ready to Make Tracks to South Carolina." The State Newspaper. Retrieved 22 December 2008. http://www.bigfootencounters.com/articles/sc.htm.

Buxton, Julian T., III, and Edward B. Macy. "The Ghosts of Charleston." Charlestonlowcountry.com. Retrieved 27 March 2009. http://www.charlestonlowcountry.com/about/ghosts.html.

Cehen, Angel. "Haunted Edisto Presbyterian Church—Edisto Island, South Carolina." Phantoms & Monsters. Retrieved 30 January 2009. http://naturalplane.blogspot.com/2009/01/haunted-edisto-presbyterian-church.html.

Bibliography

"Charleston, South Carolina." Wikipedia. 7 March 2009. http://en
.wikipedia.org/wiki/Charleston,_South_Carolina.

"Charleston: Ghostly Enchantment." Eaglelatitudes.com. Retrieved 3 January 2009. http://www.eaglelatitudes.com/current/article.html?id = 759.

"Charleston Stage Profile." Charleston Stage. Retrieved 3 January 2009. http://www.charlestonstage.com/about_us/index.php.

"City of West Columbia." Westcolumbiasc.gov. Retrieved 10 January 2009. http://www.westcolumbiasc.gov/history/

Collins, Ashleigh. "The Fate of Fenwick Hall." Rehava.com. Retrieved 6 January 2009. http://blog.rehava.com/main/preserving-fenwick-hall.

"Cool Springs, Kershaw County." South Carolina Department of Archives and History. Retrieved 24 January 2009. http://www.nationalregister
.sc.gov/kershaw/S10817728013/index.htm.

"Cool Springs Plantation." South Carolina Plantations. Retrieved 24 January 2009. http://south-carolina-plantations.com/kershaw/cool-springs.html.

Cooper, James Fenimore. "The Lake Gun." Penn State Electronic Classics. Retrieved 22 January 2009. http://www.hn.psu.edu/faculty/jmanis/ jfcooper.htm.

Devereux, Tony. "History of Hagley Estates." Hagleyestates.com. Retrieved 18 December 2008. http://www.hagleyestates.com/History.html.

"Dock Street Theater: A Local Legacy." Library of Congress. Retrieved 3 January 2009. http://www.americaslibrary.gov/cgi-bin/page.cgi/es/sc/ dock_1.

"Dock Street Theatre." City of Charleston. Retrieved 3 January 2009. http://www.charlestoncity.info/dept/content.aspx?nid = 385.

"Early History of the College." Newberry College. Retrieved 16 January 2009. http://www.newberry.edu/earlyhistory.asp.

"Earth Lights: Spooklights and Ghost Lights." Inamidst.com. Retrieved 21 December 2008. http://inamidst.com/lights/earth.

"Earthquake Booms, Seneca Guns, and Other Sounds." USGS. Retrieved 18 January 2009. http://earthquake.usgs.gov/learning/topics/booms.php.

Eblin, Jennifer. "The Grey Man and Ghosts of Pawleys Island, South Carolina." Associatedcontent.com. Retrieved 15 December 2008. http://www.associatedcontent.com/pop_print.shtml?content_type = article&contenttypei.

"1843 Battery Carriage House Inn." Hoteltravelcheck.com. Retrieved 21 January 2009. http://www.hoteltravelcheck.com/haunted-hotels-charleston
.html.

"Encounters with Alice Flagg, Ghost of the Hermitage in Murrells Inlet, South Carolina." Cleananpress.com. Retrieved 14 December 2008. http://www.cleananpress.com/lowcountry/aice.htm.

Evans, Erin. "Haunted Clemson." Thetigernews.com. Retrieved 22 December 2008. http://media.www.thetigernews.com/media/storage/ paper863/news/2005/10./28/News/Ha...

"Fenwick Hall Plantation: John's Island, South Carolina, USA."
  Fenwickhall.com. Retrieved 6 January 2009. http://www
  .fenwickhall.com.
"First Lizard Man Spotter Passes Polygraph." Bigfoot Encounters. Retrieved
  16 December 2008. http://www.bigfootencounters.com/articles/
  lizard.htm.
"Foster's Tavern, Spartanburg County." South Carolina Department of
  Archives and History. Retrieved 13 February 2009. http://www
  .nationalregister.sc.gov/spartanburg/S108177442005/index.htm.
"Garden Theatre—Charleston, SC." Scmovietheatres.com. Retrieved 27 January 2009. http://www.scmovietheatres.com/chas_gar.html.
"Ghost Stories of Hilton Head, SC." Of Graveyards and Things. Retrieved 17
  December 2008. http://mblauss.blogspot.com/2006/12/
  ghost-stories-of-hilton-head-sc.html.
"Gullah Culture in Danger of Fading Away." National Geographic. Retrieved
  1 January 2009. http://news.nationalgeographic.com/news/2001/06/
  0607_wiregullah.html.
"Hampton Plantation." South Carolina Plantations. Retrieved 7 January
  2009. http://south-carolina-plantations.com/charleston/hampton.html.
"Haunted Charleston South Carolina 70, 82." Hubpages.com. Retrieved 27
  March 2009. http://hubpages.com/hub/Haunted-Charleston-South
  -Carolina.
"Haunted Local Folklore and Legends in South Carolina." Associatedcontent
  .com. Retrieved 19 February 2009. http://www.associatedcontent.com/
  article/456581/haunted_local_folklore_and_le"Haunting gends.ht...
"Haunting at Herdklotz Park a.k.a. Greenville's Old Tuberculosis Sanitor-
  ium." Modernmindreader.com. Retrieved 19 February 2009.
  http://www.modernmindreader.com/blog/archieves/22.
"Herdklotz Park." Greenville Recreation District. Retrieved 19 February
  2009. http://www.gerd.org/herdklotz.html.
Hicks, Theresa M. "Did You Hear About . . . The Low Country Heresy?"
  Palmettoroots.org. Retrieved 9 January 2009. http://www.palmettoroots
  .org/SC_Believe_It_or_Not.html.
"History." Anderson University (SC). Retrieved 21 December 2008.
  http://www.andersonuniversity.edu/main/default.aspx?headerid = 2534
  &menuid = 44&page...
"History of Braddock's Point Plantation." Of Graveyards and Things.
  Retrieved 17 December 2008. http://mblauss.blogspot.com/2006/
  12/stoney-baynard-ruins-sea-pines-hilton.html.
"History." The Walker Foundation. Retrieved 7 February 2009.
  http://www.walkerfdn.org/history.htm.
Hollings, Ernest F. "The Dock Street Theater." Local Legacies. Retrieved 3
  January 2009. http://lcweb2.loc.gov/diglib/legacies/SC/200003498
  .html.
House, John Arthur. "Town Locations." Seaviewinn.net. Retrieved 12
  December 2008. http://seaviewinn.net/plantationtoursaturday.pdf.

Bibliography

Huntsinger, Elizabeth. "Pelican Inn of Pawleys Island." Coastalguide.com. Retrieved 15 December 2008. http://www.coastalguide.com/tales/pelicangreyman.shtml.

"In Search of South Carolina Spirits." Thestate.com. Retrieved 20 December 2008. http://www.thestate.com/living/story/569298.html.

"Inside the Gates of Historic Fenwick Hall Plantation." Preservation Society of Charleston. Retrieved 6 January 2009. http://www.preservationsociety.org/events_detail.asp?evID = 2.

"Irmo, South Carolina." Geocities.com. Retrieved 22 December 2008. http://www.geocities.com/CapitolHill/1171/irmo019.html?200822.

Kearns, Taylor. "Ghost Stories Create Rich History for Columbia Landmarks." Wistv.com. Retrieved 23 December 2008. http://www.wistv.com/global/story.asp?s = 9256209.

Kuderna, Joshua. "Mississippi: Magnolia Cotton Mills." Userpages.umbc.edu. Retrieved 10 January 2009. http://userpages.umbc.edu/~arubin/HIST402_SP2007/424D810EDE89848Cl666F35B4B9...

"Lake Murray History." Lakemurray.com. Retrieved 22 December 2008. http://www.lakemurray.com/Lake_Murray_History.aspx.

"Lake Murray (South Carolina)." Wikipedia. Retrieved 22 December 2008. http://en.wikipedia.org/wiki/Lake_Murray_(South_Carolina).

"Lavinia Fisher." Geocities.com. Retrieved 1 January 2009. http://www.geocities.com/nancie2339/laviniafisher.html?20091.

"Legends of the Grand Strand . . . Pirates and Ghosts!" Tripsmarter.com. Retrieved 14 December 2008. http://www.tripsmarter.com/myrtlebeach/archives/ghostories.htm.

"Litchfield Plantation." BookRags.com. Retrieved 23 January 2009. http://www.bookrags.com/wiki/Litchfield_Plantation.

"Litchfield Plantation." Wikipedia. Retrieved 23 January 2009. http://en.wikipedia.org/wiki/Litchfield_Plantation.

"Lizard Man of Scape Ore Swamp." Wikipedia. Retrieved 22 February 2009. http://en.wikipedia.org/wiki/Lizard_Man_of_Scape_Ore_Swamp.

"Lizard Man of South Carolina." Cryptomundo. Retrieved 16 December 2008. http://www.cryptomundo.com/bigfoot-report/sc-lizard-man/.

"Lizard Man of South Carolina returns—Video." Monstersandcritics.com. Retrieved 16 December 2008. http://www.monstersandcritics.com/people/bizarre/news/article_1393641.php/Lizard_Ma...

"'Lizard Man' Returns?" WIS10. Retrieved 16 December 2008. http://www.wistv.com/Global/story.asp?S = 7948448.

"Lizard Men." Unknown Explorers. Retrieved 22 February 2009. http://www.unknownexplorers.com/lizardmen.php.

"Longstreet Theater." Columbia Courtyard Downtown. Retrieved 25 December 2008. http://www.courtyardcolumbiausc.com/longstreet-theater.htm.

"Mary Ingleman: The First Witch of Fairfield County, South Carolina." Geocities.com. Retrieved 9 January 2009. http://www.geocities.com/kell1744/betweenworlds/witch_ingleman.html.

McCawley, Patrick. "The Gray Man of Pawleys Island." State.sc. Retrieved
15 December 2008. http://www.state.sc.us/scdah/grayman.htm.
"Medway Plantation." South Carolina Plantations. 5 January 2009.
http://south-carolina-plantations.com/berkeley/medway.html.
"Medway Plantation." South Carolina TriCounty Genealogy. Retrieved 5 January 2009. http://homepages.rootsweb.ancestry.com/ ~ tga/plantations/
medway.html.
Mikkelson, Barbara. "Just Dying to Get Out." Snopes.com. Retrieved 30 January 2009. http://www.snopes.com/horrors/gruesome/buried.asp.
Minsker, Marc. "The Third Eye Man." Midnet.sc.edu. 23 December 2008.
http://www.midnet.sc.edu/ghost/ThirdEyeMan.htm.
"Most Recent Reports: South Carolina." Bigfoot Field Researchers Organization. Retrieved 22 December 2008. http://www.bfro.net/GDB/state
_listing.asp?State = sc.
"My Experience at a Haunted Bed & Breakfast." Bukisa.com. Retrieved 9
February. http://buksiz.com/articles/11940_my-experience-at-a
-haunted-bed-and-breakfast.
"Newberry SC Ghosts 87." Hubpages.com. 16 January 2009. http://
hubpages.com/hub/Newberry_SC_Ghosts.
"Oakwood Cemetery aka Hells Gate." Forgotten US.com. Retrieved 7 February 2009. http://wwww.forgottenus.com/index.php?p = place.view&
place = 1900.
"Old Charleston Jail." S.P.I.R.I.T. Retrieved 1 January 2009. http://www
.southeasternhauntings.com/char-jail.php.
Opala, Joseph. "The Gullah." Yale.edu. Retrieved 1 January 2009. http://
www.yale.edu/glc/gullah/index.htm.
"Pawleys Island, South Carolina." Wikipedia. Retrieved 15 December 2008.
http://en.wikipedia.org/wiki/Pawleys_Island,_South_Carolina.
"Phantom Hitchhiker." Real Haunted House. Retrieved 8 January 2009.
http://www.realhaunts.com/united-states/phantom-hitchhiker/
"Phantom Horseman." Members.tripod.com. Retrieved 13 January 2009.
http://members.tripod.com/jayboy74/story24.html.
"Plantation History." Litchfieldplantation.com. Retrieved 23 January 2009.
http://www.litchfieldplantation.com/plantation.htm.
"Poogan's Porch: A New Story." Ghosttakers.com. Retrieved 3 February
2004. http://ghosttakers.com/poogan's_porch.htm.
"Poogan's Porch Restaurant." Hauntings. Retrieved 4 February 2009.
http://hauntedsites.blogspot.com/2006/11/poogans-porch-restaurant
.html.
"Presbyterian Church on Edisto Island." South Carolina Parks & Tourism.
Retrieved 30 January 2009. http://www.discoversouthcarolina.com/
products/3410.aspx.
"Provost Dungeon: Charleston, South Carolina." Graveaddiction.com.
Retrieved 1 January 2009. http://www.graveaddiction.com/duncharl
.html.

Bibliography

"Rice Hope Plantation." South Carolina Plantations. Retrieved 27 January 2009. http://south-carolina-plantations.com/berkeley/rice-hope.html.

"Saint Phillip's Church Cemetery." Find a Grave. Retrieved 3 January 2009. http://www.findagrave.com/php/famous.php?page = cem& FScemeteryid = 641366.

Seibels, Genie. "Poe on Sullivan's Island." Literary Traveler. Retrieved 2 February 2009. http://literarytraveler.com/literary_articles/poe_on _sullivans-island.aspx.

"Seneca Guns." Geocities.com. Retrieved 18 January 2009. http://www .geocities.com/captsilversteele/ghosts/seneca.html?200918.

"Some Haunted Places in Charleston, South Carolina." Associatedcontent .com. Retrieved 3 January 2009. http://www.associatedcontent.com/ article/5832/some_haunted_places_in_charleston_south...

"Sonic Boom? Earthquake? Big Bang Theories Abound." Farshores. Retrieved 18 January 2009. http://farshores.org/n03boom2.htm.

"South Carolina." Wikipedia. Retrieved 6 March 2009. http://en.wikipedia .org/wiki/South_Carolina.

"South Carolina Ghosts." Hauntedtravels.com. Retrieved 9 February 2009. http://www.hauntedtravels.com/south_%20ghosts.htm.

"South Carolina School for the Deaf and Blind." Geocities.com. Retrieved 7 February 2009. http://www.geocities.com/askyewolfe/hauntscsdb.html.

"South Carolina State Museum." ColumbiaSouthCarolina.com. Retrieved 10 January 2009. http://www.columbiasouthcarolina.com/statemuseum .html.

Stalker, Heather Dawkins. "Legendary Landmarks of College Campuses." Knowitall.org. Retrieved 21 December 2008. http://www.knowitall.org/ sandlapper/Winter-2008/PDFs/Landmarks.pdf.

"Stede Bonnet." Charleston Pirates. Retrieved 27 March 2009. http://www.charlestonpirates.com/stede_bonnet.html.

"Stede Bonnet." Sciway3.net. Retrieved 27 March 2009. http://www .sciway3.net/2001sc-pirates/bonnet.html.

"Stede Bonnet." Wikipedia. 27 March 2009. http://en.wikipedia.org/wiki/ Stede_Bonnet.

"St. Phillip's Episcopal Church—Charleston, SC." Waymarking.com. Retrieved 1 January 2009. http://waymarking.com/waymarks/ WM2WFB.

"Strawberry Chapel and Childsbury Town, Berkeley County." South Carolina Department of Archives and History. Retrieved 27 January 2009. http://www.nationalregister.sc.gov/berkeley/S10817708023/index.htm.

"Summerville Light." Castle of Spirits Ghost Story. Retrieved 6 January 2009. http://www.castleofspirits.com/summerville.html.

"Summerville Light NightCache." Geocaching.com. Retrieved 6 January 2009. http://www.geocaching.com/seek/chace_details.aspx?guid = e4dbb535-ee8f-4532-99a7-9f511.

"Summerville Light Road (South Carolina)." Unsolved Mysteries. Retrieved 6 January 2009. http://www.unsolvedmysteries.com/usm66559.html.

"Summerville, South Carolina." Wikipedia. Retrieved 6 January 2009.
   http://en.wikipedia.org/wiki/Sumerville,_South_Carolina.
"The Garden Theater (1918-2004)." Cinematreasures.org. Retrieved 27 January 2009. http://cinematreasures.org/news/11730_0_1_0_C/.
"The Geography of South Carolina." Netstate.com. Retrieved 6 March 2009.
   http://www.netstate.com/states/geography/sc_geography.htm.
"The Ghost of Poogan's Porch." Sciway2.net. Retrieved 4 February 2009.
   http://sciway2.net/2002/a27p/.
"The Ghosts of the Old Exchange & Provost Dungeon in Charleston, South
   Carolina." Associatedcontent.com. Retrieved 1 January 2009. http://www
   .associatedcontent.com/article/306884/the_ghosts_of_the_old_exchange
   _provost...
"The Gray Man." Haunted Lowcountry. Retrieved 15 December 2008.
   http://www.hauntedlowcountry.com/index.php?hauntlow/south
   _carolina/the_gray_man/
"The Gray Man." Sciway2.net. Retrieved 15 December 2008. http://sciway2
   .net/2002/a85b/gray;man.htm.
"The Grey Man Origin." The Moonlit Road. Retrieved 15 December 2008.
   http://www.themoonlitroad.com/archives/grayman/grayman
   _cbg001.html.
"The Grey Man of Pawley's Island." Century 21 at the Beach. Retrieved 15
   December 2008. http://pawleysisland.wordpress.com/2007/10/19/
   the-grey-man-of-pawleys-island/.
"The Grey Man Pawleys Island." Southcarolinaghost.tripod.com. Retrieved
   15 December 2008. http://southcarolinaghost.tripd.com/GhostStories/
   id27.html.
"The Hermitage—Alice Allard—A Story of Unrequited Love." Haunted Lowcountry. Retrieved 14 December 2008. http://www.hauntedlowcountry
   .com/index.php?Hauntlow/south_carolina/alice_allard
"The History of the Old Exchange." Oldexchange.com. 27 March 2009.
   http://www.oldexchange.com/html/history.html.
"The Hopewell Tuberculosis Sanitorium." Strangeusa.com. Retrieved 19
   February 2009. http://www.strangeusa.com/ViewLocation.aspx
   ?locationid = 8967.
"The Hound of Goshen: South Carolina." Tripod.com. Retrieved 20 December 2008. http://members.tripod.com/jayboy74/story76.html.
"The Inn at Meridun: An Antebellum Country Inn." Meridun.com. Retrieved
   9 February 2009. http://www.meridun.com/history.html.
"The Inn at Meridun—Haunted Bed and Breakfast." About.com. Retrieved
   13 February 2009. http://bandb.about.com/b/2007/10/22/the-inn-at
   -meridun-haunted-bed-and-breakfast.htm.
"The First Unitarian Church in the South." Charlestonuu.org. Retrieved 1
   February 2009. http://www.charlestonuu.org/History/tabid/155/
   Default.aspx.
"The Legend of the Blue Lady." CQ's Restaurant. Retrieved 18 December
   2008. http://www.cqrestaurant.com/the_legend_of_the_blue_lady.html.

Bibliography

"The Lizard-Man of Bishopville, South Carolina." Reptoids Research Center. Retrieved 16 December 2008. http://www.reptoids.com/Vault/Bishopville.htm.

"The Phantom Horseman of Columbia." Midnet.sc.edu. Retrieved 13 January 2009. http://www.midnet.sc.edu/ghost/horse.htm.

"The Provost Dungeon." Oldexchange.com. Retrieved 1 January 2009. http://www.oldexchange.com/html.Dungeon.html.

"The Stories of Poogan's Porch." Sciway2.net. Retrieved 4 February 2009. http://sciway2.net/2007/a27p/story.html.

"The Swamp Girl." Midnet.sc.edu. Retrieved 21 December 2008. http://www.midnet.sc.edu/ghost/swamp.htm.

"The Wedgefield Ghost." Wedgefield Plantation. Retrieved 7 January 2009. http://www.wedgefield.com/wedgefield_ghost.htm.

"Three Ghost Encounters." X/Stories. Retrieved 7 February 2009. http://www.wirenot.net/X/Stories/GhostF_2/Ghost_T/threeghostencounters.shtml.

Trull, D. "The Boy Who Cried Bigfoot—Shady Sasquatch Sighting in South Carolina." Sightings in South Carolina. http://www.bigfootencounters.com/stories/south_carolina.htm.

"25 Years Ago, Ghost Reported on Anderson University Campus." Independentmail.com. Retrieved 21 December 2008. http://www.independentmail.com/news/2007/oct/30/25-years-ago-ghost-reported-anderson.

"Unitarian Churchyard." Graveaddiction.com. Retrieved 1 February 2009. http://www.graveaddiction.com/unitarch.html.

"Wade Hampton." Capitol Complex. Retrieved 17 January 2009. http://www.aoc.gov/cc/art/nsh/hampton.cfm.

"Wade Hampton III." Wikipedia. Retrieved 17 January 2009. http://en.wikipedia.org/wiki/Wade_hampton_III.

Warren, Joshua P. "Report on Investigation of the Charleston, SC Old City Jail." L.E.M.U.R. Retrieved 1 January 2009. http://shadowboxent.brinkster.net/LEMUR/charlestonoldcityjail.html.

"Why Did Poe Write Annabel Lee?" Greenspun.com. Retrieved 2 February 2009. http://www.greenspun.com/bboard/q-and-a-fetch-msg.tcl?msg_id = 0033EU.

Newspaper and Journal Articles

Foxworth, Eleanor Winn. "The Ghosts of Goshen Hill." *Sandlapper*. Autumn 2007: 12–13.

Thomas, W. H. J. "Home in South Battery Represents Two Periods." *Charlotte News and Courier*. 20 October 1969.

Personal Interviews

Connor, Kathy Jo. Interviewed by the author. 27 July 2004.

Edens, Lou. Interviewed by the author. 25 July 2004.

Feind, Jane M. Interviewed by the author. 27 July 2004.

Acknowledgments

THE COMPLETION OF THIS BOOK WOULD NOT HAVE BEEN POSSIBLE without the contributions of a number of people. The generous financial support provided by the University of West Alabama's University Research Grants committee made it possible for me to collect ghost stories in South Carolina. I am very grateful to Kathy Jo Connor, Lou Edens, and Jane M. Feind for granting me interviews while I visited the state. As usual, my wife, Marilyn accompanied me on my trip and used her "ghostly magnetism" to activate a number of the spirits. At Stackpole Books, I am grateful to production editor Brett Keener for enhancing the readability of the book. Finally, I am indebted to acquisitions editor Kyle Weaver for putting up with my eccentricities and for encouraging me to write these books.

About the Author

ALAN BROWN IS A PROFESSOR OF ENGLISH AT THE UNIVERSITY OF WEST Alabama in Livingston. Brown has written extensively about the folklore and ghost stories of the South. He is the author of *Haunted Kentucky, Haunted Georgia, Haunted Texas,* and *Haunted Tennessee.* When he is not teaching or writing, Brown gives ghost tours of the city of Livingston and UWA's campus.

Other Titles in the
Haunted Series
by Alan Brown

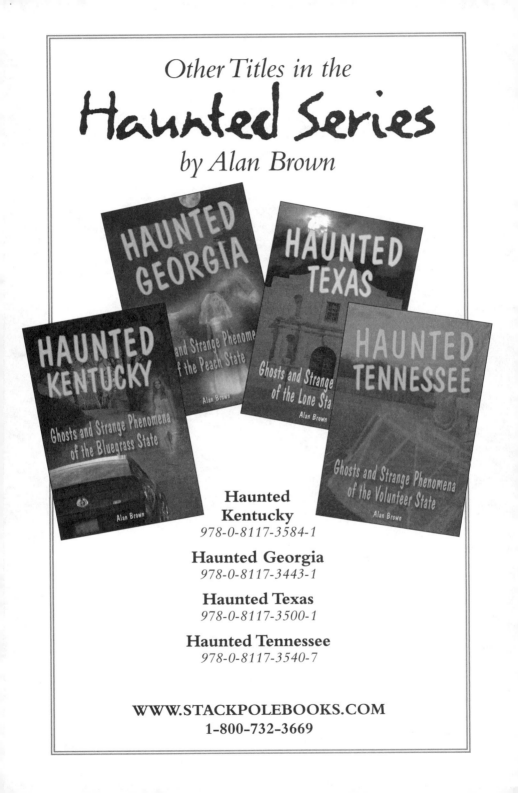

**Haunted
Kentucky**
978-0-8117-3584-1

Haunted Georgia
978-0-8117-3443-1

Haunted Texas
978-0-8117-3500-1

Haunted Tennessee
978-0-8117-3540-7

Other Titles in the
Haunted Series

Haunted Connecticut
by Cheri Revai • *978-0-8117-3296-3*
Haunted Delaware
by Patricia A. Martinelli • *978-0-8117-3297-0*
Haunted Florida
by Cynthia Thuma and Catherine Lower
978-0-8117-3498-1
Haunted Illinois
by Troy Taylor • *978-0-8117-3499-8*
Haunted Maine
by Charles A. Stansfield Jr. • *978-0-8117-3373-1*
Haunted Maryland
by Ed Okonowicz • *978-0-8117-3409-7*
Haunted Massachusetts
by Cheri Revai • *978-0-8117-3221-5*
Haunted New Jersey
by Patricia A. Martinelli and Charles A. Stansfield Jr.
978-0-8117-3156-0
Haunted New York
by Cheri Revai • *978-0-8117-3249-9*
Haunted New York City
by Cheri Revai • *978-0-8117-3471-4*
Haunted Ohio
by Charles A. Stansfield Jr. • *978-0-8117-3472-1*
Haunted Pennsylvania
by Mark Nesbitt and Patty A. Wilson
978-0-8117-3298-7
Haunted West Virginia
by Patty A. Wilson • *978-0-8117-3400-4*

WWW.STACKPOLEBOOKS.COM • 1-800-732-3669